The Santa Cruz Mountains Trail Book

by Tom Taber

FIFTH EDITION

The Parks and Trails of the mountains of San Mateo, Santa Clara, and Santa Cruz counties.

The Oak Valley Press

ISBN 0-9609170-3-9

First Edition 1976
Second Edition 1979
Third Edition 1982
Fourth Edition 1985

Maps by Tom Taber and Bob Newey
Illustrations, cover, and design by Tom Taber.

Photo Credits:
Eileen Snider: Page 40
Sempervirens Fund: Page 121
Tree Top Challenges: Page 105
Tom Taber: Pages 1, 4, 7, 15, 18, 23, 24, 29, 30, 32, 36, 38, 43, 46, 47, 52, 59, 62, 64, 68, 70, 72, 75, 79, 84, 85, 88, 89, 91, 93, 95, 97, 107, 109, 112, 116, 117, 123, 125, 127, 130.

THE OAK VALLEY PRESS
228 Virginia Ave.,
San Mateo, CA 94402

Table of Contents:

SPECIAL SECTIONS:

Introduction

About every 3 years it becomes apparent that there are enough new parks and trails to require a new edition of this book. This is especially true of this edition, which includes more substantial changes than ever before.

In addition to 10 new parks and preserves and countless major and minor changes in previously described public lands, I have also added some special sections that should be of interest to trail users. Among these are discussions about dealing with poison oak and ticks, information on walking for health, descriptions of natural and human history, a recipe for acorn muffins, a listing of places to walk your dog, a section for off-road bicyclists, and a call for more volunteer trail builders.

Many of the new trails and parks are the result of hard work by hundreds of volunteers, with a shovel or a pen, who got involved when it mattered. Cascade Ranch, for example, would now be an expensive subdivision instead of a new state park if not for an aggressive campaign by local conservationists.

The new preserves of the Midpeninsula Regional Open Space District are also the result of citizen activists who originally put the idea of open space on the ballot and the voters who made it a reality.

Don't ever think that the Bay Area's extraordinary greenbelt legacy—the best in the country—is a gift from the government. It isn't; and in fact many of the best places were preserved over the kicking and screaming of politicians from the local to the federal level.

The future is also up to you, the public. Should there be a campground and conference center at Cascade Ranch State Park? Should Highway 1 be re-routed through the middle of McNee Ranch State Park?

(Continued on page 10)

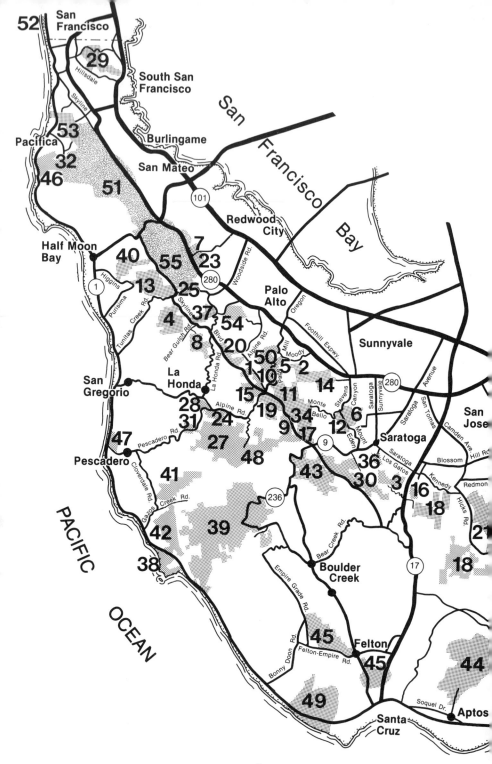

OPEN SPACE PRESERVES

1 Coal Creek
2 Duveneck Windmill Pasture
3 El Sereno
4 El Corte de Madera Creek
5 Foothills
6 Fremont Older
7 Hassler
8 La Honda Creek
9 Long Ridge
10 Los Trancos
11 Monte Bello
12 Picchetti Ranch
13 Purisima Creek Redwoods
14 Rancho San Antonio
15 Russian Ridge
16 Saint Joseph's Hill
17 Saratoga Gap
18 Sierra Azul
19 Skyline Ridge
20 Windy Hill

COUNTY PARKS

21 Almaden Quicksilver
22 Calero Reservoir
23 Edgewood
24 Heritage Grove
25 Huddart
26 Mount Madonna
27 Pescadero Creek
28 Sam McDonald
29 San Bruno Mountain
30 Sanborn Skyline
31 San Mateo Memorial
32 San Pedro Valley
33 Santa Teresa
34 Skyline
35 Uvas Canyon
36 Villa Montalvo
37 Wunderlich

STATE PARKS

38 Año Nuevo
39 Big Basin Redwoods
40 Burleigh Murray Ranch
41 Butano
42 Cascade Ranch
43 Castle Rock
44 Forest of Nisene Marks
45 Henry Cowell Redwoods
46 NcNee Ranch
47 Pescadero Marsh
48 Portola
49 Wilder Ranch

CITY PARKS

50 Foothills
51 San Francisco Fish and
   Game Refuge

GOLDEN GATE NATIONAL RECREATION AREA

52 Fort Funston
53 Sweeney Ridge

PRIVATE

54 Jasper Ridge Biological Preserve
55 Filoli Estate

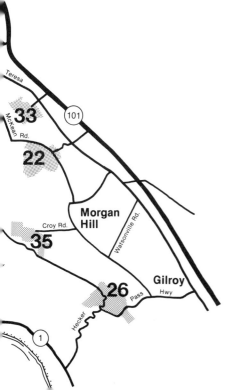

Continued from page 7

Should off-road bicycles be prohibited from some trails? And which ones? Should a golf course cover part of Edgewood County Park? Can a trail connection between Long Ridge Open Space and Portola State Park be negotiated? Should there be walk-in campsites at Burleigh Murray Ranch State Park? How much visitor development should be allowed at Skyline Ridge Open Space?

These and many other questions await decision in the next few years.

The Value of Wildlands

There is a dangerous myth going around that natural places aren't important. It is based on the false assumption that some things in Nature are superfluous.

The Earth is a living and self-regulating biological system. Its atmosphere is a reactive mixture of gasses created and sustained by life. Every time you take a breath your survival depends on the metabolic activity of millions of species of plants and animals. This vast genetic diversity is essential for the whole system to function. The more pieces we remove the less stable it is.

For this reason our wildlands are more than just places of scenery and recreation. They are elements of Earth's life-support system, and they are more productive and necessary than freeways, subdivisions, golf courses, or anything else man can build.

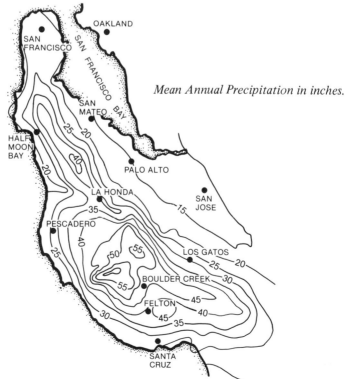

Mean Annual Precipitation in inches.

The Santa Cruz Mountains

Geography and Climate

The Santa Cruz Mountains are a range of parallel, northwest-tending ridges extending for about 80 miles from San Bruno Mountain to the Pajaro River. It is narrowest and lowest on the San Francisco peninsula, getting wider, higher, and wilder to the south. The highest peak is 3,800 foot high Loma Prieta, though only a few peaks exceed 3,000 feet.

Deep layers of sedimentary rock, called the Franciscan Formation, were deposited nearly 100 million years ago when this whole area was below the ocean. For incomprehensible ages the land rose and fell. At the time of the Miocene upheavels—about 10 million years ago—it was raised above the sea in northwest-tending ridges as we find it today. Periodic volcanic activity spewed out igneous rock, and to further complicate matters the range was sliced across by several faults, the largest and most famous being the San Andreas.

One of the first things you will notice about the Santa Cruz Mountains is the close relationship between the ocean and the climate. Notice how much greener they are than the Diablo range in the East Bay Area, and how much greener and more forested is the west side of the range than the east side. This range has a coastal marine climate, with rainless summers and greatest moisture—often in the form of fog— on the seaward side of the mountains. Cool, moist marine air sweeps eastward off the ocean and piles up on the mountains' western slopes.

Precipitation varies from more than 40 inches in the Butano and Big Basin area to only about 11 inches in the "rainshadow" in the Santa Clara Valley. Mean maximum summer temperatures range from 70 to 75 degrees fahrenheit during August and September. The minimum temperatures vary from 36 to 40 degrees fahrenheit in January. Snowfall on the higher peaks and ridges is rare and short-lived, and hiking is great in any season. The brown-gold season and the green season each have their own distinct character that adds an appealing diversity to coastal California.

The ideal place for redwoods to grow is away from the brisk ocean winds, but on the seaward side of the range where the coastal fog can cool and dampen the forest. They also like deep, shady canyon bottoms where streams retain moisture all through the dry season. You might also notice that redwoods prefer the shady north-facing slopes where exposure to sunlight is reduced and can't rob the great trees of precious moisture.

During the early spring months a cool air mass called the "Pacific High" gathers north of Hawaii and west of San Francisco. It hits the California coast in a southeasterly course and pushes great quantities of water along the coast. This moist air mass is cooled by contact with deep upwelling water and condenses in the form of fog, which is deflected by the coast range and usually only penetrates the continent at low mountain passes.

Ecology

Notice the relationship between plants and their environment. Oak and madrone are examples of sun-loving trees found on dry ridgetops and on the sunny southside of hills. Chaparral plants such as chamise, sage, manzanita, and scrub oak, grow on the driest parts of the range and are characterized by small leaves and deep roots to conserve moisture. Oak trees are also deep-rooted and have drought-resistant leaves. One of the most noticeable seasonal changes occurs in the grasslands, which change from green to gold as the rains come and go.

Close to 150 species of grasses grow in the Santa Cruz Mountains, though it soon becomes obvious that some species are a lot more common than others. The perennial bunch grasses that once covered these hills have been mostly replaced by the European annuals, which were brought here in the hooves and fur of livestock. The new grasses were so successful they completely changed the character of these hills.

The amazing thing about this herbaceous revolution is that the introduced species were better adapted to survival in California's drought cycle than the natives. The reason for this is that the foreign invaders — the foxtails, fescues, wild oats, and downy chess, to name a few — had several advantages over the bunch grasses: 1) they grow more quickly than the native perennials; 2) they use the winter and spring rainfall more efficiently by growing quickly and then by turning brown to wait out the summer drought.

Notice the fire scars on many old redwoods, evidence of forest fires that swept through the mountains long before Europeans entered the area. Fire actually benefits redwoods by removing competing plants and by exposing minerals soil which is essential to the germination of seedlings. Redwoods are often hollowed out by fire, but their thick and nonresinous bark usually helps them survive and recover. Most redwood reproduction is through sprouting from the roots of existing trees. Notice the kind of plants that cover the redwood forest floor. Ferns, sorrel, wild ginger, and many other beautiful plants thrive in the moist and dark parts of the forest. Notice how sorrel avoids direct sunlight. The leaves lower against the stem — like a butterfly at rest — when struck by sunlight.

Manzanita

12

Almaden Quicksilver County Park

TO GET THERE. . . take Almaden Expressway south to the town of New Almaden. The Mine Hill Trail begins at the dirt road off to the west just north of Alamitos Creek. Or you can take Almaden Expressway south from San Jose, turn west on Camden and south on McAbee to the end of the road.

This roomy 3,570 acre park, with 30 miles of trails, is open exclusively for hikers and equestrians and is a great place to see wildlife.

Turkey vultures often cruise the air currents here, with a sharp eye for anything that might be dead. With a wingspan sometimes exceeding 6 feet, this is one of the Bay Area's largest birds, and can be recognized by their red, naked heads and black feathers. One blistering hot day in September I sprawled out in the shade of a solitary oak on a grassy hillside, maneuvering around for a comfortable position for a short nap. Soon I noticed an inquisitive vulture circling overhead. A few minutes later another one joined the aerial investigation, and by the time a third bird joined the group I lost my desire for sleep. I still wonder how long it takes for a sleeping hiker to be declared dead.

From the Almaden Road entrance, take the Mine Hill Trail uphill for sweeping views as you climb to an altitude exceeding 1,500 feet and then loop back via the Randal Mine Trail. This is an all-day hike with some strenuous grades and passes through grasslands, chaparral, and oak woodlands. From the McAbee Road entrance combine the Mine Hill and Guadalupe trails for an easy hike that loops over a ridge and past Guadalupe Reservoir.

From the McAbee Road trailhead you can walk an easy and scenic 7-mile loop by combining the Mine Hill and Guadalupe trails. Remnants of the quicksilver (mercury) mining that was the base of the local economy are seen. Quicksilver was discovered by Mexican Cavalry captain Andres Castillero in 1845, and this soon became one of the great quicksilver producing areas of the world. As the ore was depleted, however, the thriving mining communities became ghost towns, and the Quicksilver Mining Company declared bankruptcy in 1912.

Situated on the dry east side of the range, the park is covered mostly with oak woods and grasslands, which change from golden brown in summer and autumn to green in the winter and spring. The elevation ranges from less than 400 feet to more than 1,600 feet. If you want to do some rock climbing test your skills on Guadalupe Rock, at the upstream end of Guadalupe Reservoir. During the wet season the base of the rock is often submerged.

This park, only 11 miles south of San Jose, is open from 8 a.m. until sundown. For more information, call the Santa Clara County Parks and Recreation Department at (408) 358-3751.

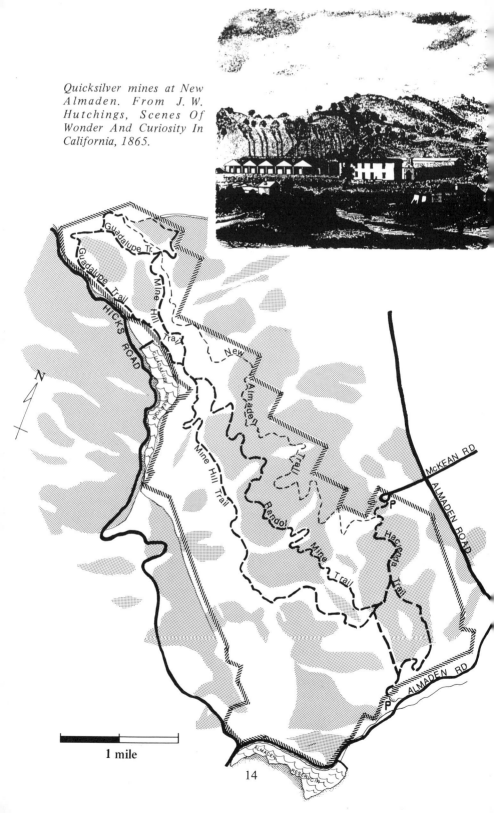

Quicksilver mines at New Almaden. From J. W. Hutchings, Scenes Of Wonder And Curiosity In California, 1865.

14

Ano Nuevo State Reserve

TO GET THERE . . . take New Years Creek Road off Highway 1 about 19 miles north of Santa Cruz.

Año Nuevo is truly one of America's great marine wildlife preserves.

Cormorants nest on ocean cliffs, tidepools abound with intertidal life, sea lions, fur seals, and harbor seals are commonly seen and heard on the beaches and rocks here, and even sea otters are sited more often every year. But the preserve is most popular from December through March when a colony of elephant seals visits the island and peninsula for mating and bearing young. To protect these enormous mammals, and the people who come to see them, the preserve is open only through naturalist guided tours at this time of the year.

Male elephant seals arrive in December to establish a breeding hierarchy and are followed in January by the females who join the harems of the dominant males. Male seals are enormous, reaching lengths of 16 feet and weighing 3 tons. Females are much smaller, at 1,200 to 2,000 pounds. Slaughtered for their oil-rich blubber, by 1892 less than 100 remained. In the 1920s the Mexican and United States governments gave them legal protection, allowing their numbers to rapidly increase since then. They first returned to Año Nuevo Island in 1955 and are now also breeding on the peninsula. These animals, the largest members of the seal family, seem awkward on land, but they are excellent swimmers, able to dive as deep as 1,000 feet to feed mainly on rays, squids, skates, and fish.

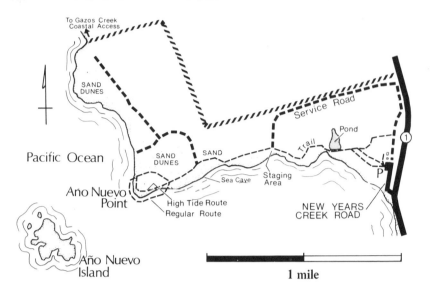

To Gazos Creek
Coastal Access

SAND
DUNES

Service Road

Pacific Ocean

SAND
DUNES

SAND

Trail

Pond

1

Ano Nuevo
Point

Sea Cave

Staging
Area

P

High Tide Route
Regular Route

NEW YEARS
CREEK ROAD

Año Nuevo
Island

1 mile

This fascinating peninsula is worth exploring all year; and in fact, can be most enjoyable when most of the elephant seals and their hordes of loyal admirers are gone, and walking may be done without ranger escort. Año Nuevo is one of the few places on the San Mateo County coast where it is possible to do some real hiking west from Highway 1.

Follow the trail west from the parking area, passing coastal scrub, a beautiful springtime display of wildflowers, and a small marshy pond. A little over half way to the point a wonderful sea cave invites exploration at low tide for those hardy enough to make their way down the steep embankment. Continue over the dunes and along the beach to the end of the peninsula, which is just over a mile from the parking lot, depending on your route.

Half a mile off the peninsula is 12-acre Año Nuevo Island, breeding ground for elephant seals, California and steller sea lions, and harbor seals, and a nesting place for western gulls, pigeon guillemots, and black oystercatchers. Because of its importance to coastal wildlife, public access to the island is prohibited. This cherty shale island was part of the mainland until relatively recently in geologic time, when it was separated by wave erosion and by the gradual rising of the sea level when the ice age glaciers melted over the last ten thousand years.

This area was uplifted from the sea a mere 70-100 thousand years

Park rangers and students from the University of California at Santa Cruz conduct tours of the preserve when elephant seals are here in their greatest numbers between December and March. As of this writing, tickets are available from Ticketron. Because of the popularity of these tours, be sure to get your tickets as early as possible. For more information, call the state parks office at (415) 879-0227.

16

ago — practically yesterday to geologists — creating treacherous rocky obstacles for ships. Several major shipwrecks resulted in the construction of a lighthouse on the island in 1890. Difficult to maintain, the storm-battered station was replaced by an automated signal buoy south of the island in 1948. Today, the weathered lightkeepers' house still stands clearly visible from the mainland, now inhabited only by seals, sea lions, and birds.

Tidepools exposed near the tip of the peninsula have an extraordinary abundance of marine life. Sea stars, hermit crabs, chitons, anemonies, sea urchins and many other intertidal life forms are common; and at low tide you may see what appears to be spherical boulders several feet in diameter fastened to these tidepool rocks. Closer inspection will reveal that these objects, covered with countless tiny holes, are actually tube masses, created by calciferous tube worms. Nourished largely by sea lion and seal wastes, the waters of Año Nuevo have some of the world's largest tube worm formations. Each calcium carbonate tube mass is a community of worms and a vast network of tubal tunnels.

Harbor seals are often seen lounging on the rocks offshore, and are seen bobbing their heads above water near the shore to examine humans. Their short, plump, spotted bodies are easily identified. They mate on the island in April and May.

Humans have been visiting this area for thousands of years, as evidenced by shell mounds left by a once large Ohlone Indian habitation. For many centuries Indians lived a relatively easy life, thriving on the coast's abundance of seafood, game, acorns, and other wild edibles, and had no need for agriculture. Their discarded seashells form numerous shell mounds on this peninsula. The Indians lived in lodges usually made of willow branches arranged in 6-foot circles, bent and tied at the top, and thatched and sealed with mud.

Año Nuevo has one of the oldest place names in the country, named "La Punta De Año Nuevo" (The Point Of The New Year) by the Spanish explorer Sebastian Vizcaino on January 3, 1603. Año Nuevo Bay was used for shipping redwood timber from the Santa Cruz Mountains between 1853 and 1920, and the peninsula and vicinity was part of a cattle ranch established by Isaac Steele. The old ranger residence at the parking lot was built in 1870 for Isaac's daughter, Flora Dickerman Steele. Just north are other restored ranch buildings which now house a visitors' center and bookstore.

From J.W. Hutchings, Scenes of Wonder and Curiosity In California, 1865.

Big Basin Redwoods State Park

TO GET THERE... take **Highway 9 and turn west on Highway 236. The southern access is from Boulder Creek.**

Big Basin is a large and diverse land of dark redwood groves, sunny ridges, and rocky peaks. This is the largest park in the Santa Cruz Mountains, with enough miles of trails to satisfy the most enthusiastic of hikers. Here you will find more than 45 miles of trails, which allow hikers to escape the crowded paved areas and explore some of the mountains' most beautiful semi-wilderness.

The wildest and most spectacular hike in Big Basin is the 12-mile Berry Creek-Sunset trail loop. Take an entire day and enjoy the waterfalls and remote first-growth redwood groves, stopping often to appreciate the wonderful variety of scenery. This is not an easy hike, and it has plenty of ups and downs to encourage you to slow down and enjoy your rambles. The trail has a million rewards any time of year, but most people like it best in the late winter and early spring when everything is fresh and green and Berry Creek and Silver falls are awesome torrents, plunging more than 50 feet over mossy and fern-adorned sandstone cliffs. Upstream is Golden Falls, named for the coloring of its 20 foot sandstone escarpment.

The 'Berry Creek and Sunset trails wander far from the park's crowded paved areas and pass through all the region's ecological communities. To find this route, take the Redwood Trail past the campfire circle to Opal Creek Trail, which connects with the Berry Creek and Sunset trails. Allow at least 6 hours of hiking to cover this trail. You can make a 2 day hike out of this route by camping at Sunset Trail-

camp a short distance across Berry Creek on the Sunset Trail. It is about 5.5 miles from park headquarters.

The Howard King Trail can be taken as a longer and more strenuous alternative to the Berry Creek Falls Trails. Take the Hihn Hammond dirt road up 1,840 foot high McAbee Mountain and turn right on the trail. This route has some great views, especially of the Waddell Creek canyon to the southwest.

The trail to Pine Mountain and Buzzards Roost is a strenuous but scenic 5 mile round trip climb of more than 1,000 feet from park headquarters. The climb to the 2,208 foot summit of Pine Mountain is a journey above the redwoods to an ecological island of madrone, knobcone pine, and chapparal. The weathered sandstone summit of Buzzards Roost offers the best views of the two peaks. To take this hike, follow the Opal Creek Trail south and turn right on Pine Mountain Trail. Be sure to bring water, as there is none available on the peaks.

The knobcone pine is well suited for these dry and rocky ridgetops. It is found mostly in dry areas with poor soil, where most other trees do poorly. This hardy pine needs the direct sunlight of hilltops and ridges and is dependent on fire to remove competing vegetation and for generating sufficient heat to release seeds from the cones. Put one of the cones in your oven and watch it open up and expel its seeds as the heat rises. You will also see knobcone pines on the Sunset Trail.

There is a strenuous one-day hike, or a moderate two-day backpacking trip on a scenic and diverse 14-mile loop trail through the park's northern mountains. From park headquarters walk the Opal Creek Trail upstream (north) and take the "Skyline-to-the-Sea" trail east to China Grade Road or Rim Trail, which climbs north and west to the new Lane Sunset trailcamp, built with a grant from Lane Publishing. This is a spectacular place to spend a night, with a remote wilderness feel to it. Call park headquarters for reservations. To complete the loop follow the ridge westward to the Johansen Road and the Middle Ridge Trail, which is actually a dirt road. It follows a scenic ridge southbound, past Ocean View Summit. Take Sunset Trail east to the Opal Creek Trail and back to park headquarters. This hike passes through all the park's ecological zones and involves a climb of more than 1,300 feet. Don't forget to bring drinking water, especially in summer.

If that one is too tough, you might want to go to the other extreme and take the easiest trail in the park. Just west of the parking lot near park headquarters is Redwood Trail, an easy self-guiding nature loop by some of the largest trees in the park. The trail is less than a mile long and makes an easy family stroll.

Big Basin Redwoods State Park has facilities for trail and car camping, fishing, a grocery store, and a nature museum. For more information and camping reservations, call park headquarters at (408) *338-6132.*

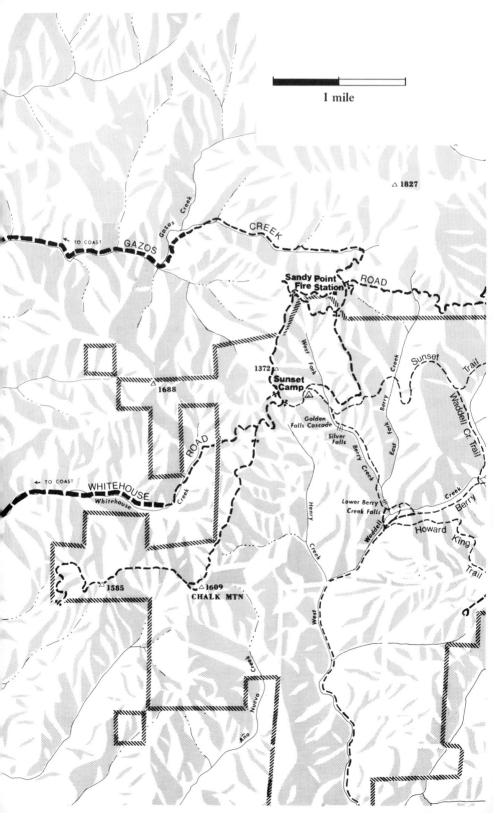

△ 1827

1 mile

TO COAST → GAZOS CREEK CREEK

Sandy Point
Fire Station
ROAD

West Fork

△ 1372
Sunset
Camp

Golden
Falls Cascade
Silver
Falls

Sunset
Trail

Berry Creek

East Fork

Waddell Cr. Trail

△ 1688

ROAD

Creek

← TO COAST WHITEHOUSE

Whitehouse

Henry Creek

Lower Berry
Creek Falls

Waddell

Creek

Berry

Howard

King
Trail

△ 1585

△ 1609
CHALK MTN

West

Creek

Nuevo

Año

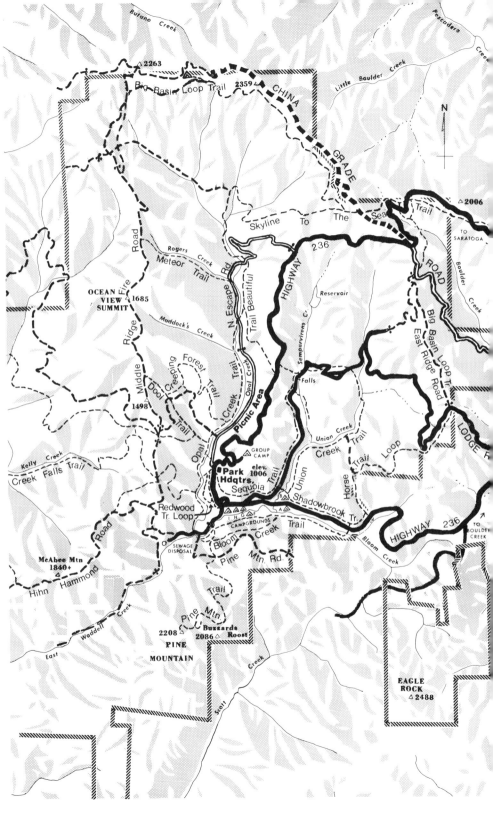

Rancho Del Oso

TO GET THERE. . . The entrance road intersects Highway 1 just south of Waddell Creek, about 18 miles northwest of Santa Cruz. It's south of Año Nuevo State Preserve.

The southern part of Big Basin Redwoods State Park stretches all the way to the ocean, encompassing the broad valley of Waddell Creek. Called Rancho Del Oso (Spanish for "Ranch of the Bear"), this area offers a beautiful stream, forests of second-growth redwood, Douglas fir, and Monterey pine, as well as meadows and a freshwater marsh.

There are 3 easily accessible trail camps in this valley. Leave your car at the parking lot near the Rancho Del Oso Nature and History Center and backpack in about 1 mile to Alder Camp, 1.2 miles to Twin Redwoods Camp, and 2.5 miles to Camp Herbert. Sunset Camp is 6.8 miles. Make trail camp reservations by calling park headquarters at (408) 338-6132 at least 2 weeks in advance for summer weekend use. Ground fires are prohibited.

If you are taking the "Skyline-to-the-Sea" trail from Big Basin park headquarters, the distance to Camp Herbert is 7.5 miles, Twin Redwoods is 9 miles, Alder Camp is 9.8 miles, and Highway 1 is about 11 miles.

This canyon was explored by Captain Gaspar de Portola in October 1769 when his scurvey-plagued expedition paused for 3 days of recuperation. Because of their rapid recovery the crew dubbed this place "Cañada de la Salud" (Canyon of Health). William Waddell came to the canyon in 1862 and built a lumber mill at the confluence of the East and West forks of Waddell Creek.

Help Build A Trail!

Every spring since 1969, volunteers have hit the trails of the Santa Cruz Mountains with shovels, picks, and trimmers to undo winter's damage and to build new trails. This tradition has been so successful that it is the model for a similar statewide event.

With tight budgets for public agencies, Trail Days—and smaller trail projects throughout the year—are essential to keeping these mountains accessible.

Coordinating these trail activities is The Trail Center, a coalition of organizations including the Sempervirens Fund, The Santa Cruz Mountains Trail Association, the Midpeninsula Regional Open Space District, and state and county parks departments.

If you would like to help, contact the Center at 4898 El Camino Real, Office 205A, Los Altos, CA 94022; (415) 968-7065.

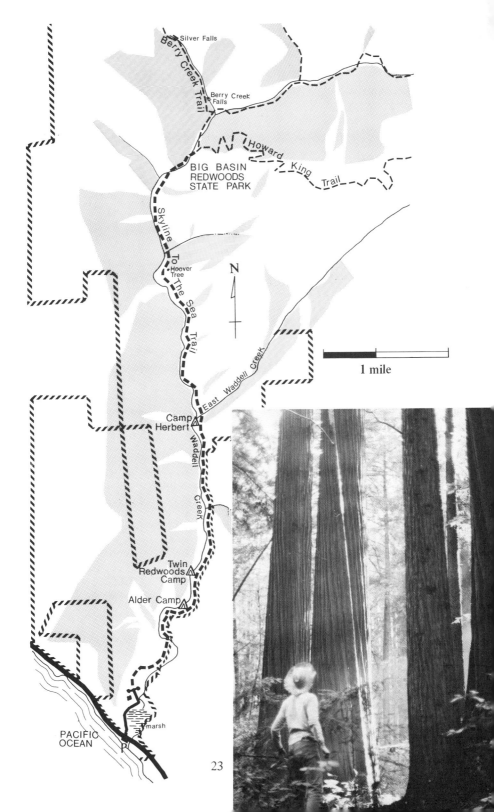

Silver Falls

Berry Creek Trail

Berry Creek Falls

Howard

BIG BASIN
REDWOODS
STATE PARK

King
Trail

Skyline

To
Hoover
Tree

The

N

Sea

Trail

East Waddell Creek

1 mile

Camp
Herbert

Waddell

Creek

Twin
Redwoods
Camp

Alder Camp

PACIFIC
OCEAN

marsh
pl

23

Burleigh Murray Ranch State Park

TO GET THERE. . . take Highway 1 just south of Half Moon Bay and turn east on Higgins Road. The dirt road trail into the park intersects Higgins Road next to "The Orchard Field", 1.6 miles from Highway 1.

Please Note: *There will be no access to this park until a planned parking lot on Higgins Road is built. For current information, call the state parks office in Half Moon Bay at (415) 726-6203*

Mills Creek tumbles more than a thousand feet down the steep western slopes of Cahill Ridge, at Skyline Boulevard, and then meanders through a broad and gentle valley as it approaches Higgins Road.

This perennial stream flows through the middle of this 1,325-acre state park, which is just 2 watersheds north of redwood-forested Purisima Creek Open Space Preserve. But unlike Purisima, the hills and mountains of Burleigh Murray are covered mainly with that combination of low bushes and vines known as coastal scrub, as well as with grasslands and scattered groves of eucalyptus. Creeks are clearly defined by narrow riperian woodlands.

Because this is ideal rabbit and rodent habitat, bobcats and coyotes abound. Birds of prey are commonly seen, including a variety of hawks and owls. Barn owls and swallows nest in the large dilapidated barn.

As of this writing, the only real trail in this park is the ranch road along Mills Creek, which is a well-maintained dirt road between Higgins Road and the house. Past the barn it more resembles a real trail, and beyond the water tanks it rapidly deteriorates, becoming progressively more difficult to follow through the scrub. There are several road cuts that have the potential of forming an excellent trail system once a route is cut through the brush. In addition to trails the park department also has plans for walk-in campsites.

From the Mills Creek ranch road you will see a cave in a sandstone outcropping high on the valley's south facing slope. It looks large and accessible from the trail, but a bushwhacking ordeal to near the ridgetop made me wish I had left my curiosity at home that day. I found the entrance to this shallow cave to be well-guarded by a steep and dangerous rocky slope.

This park was donated to the state by its former owner, rancher Burleigh Murray.

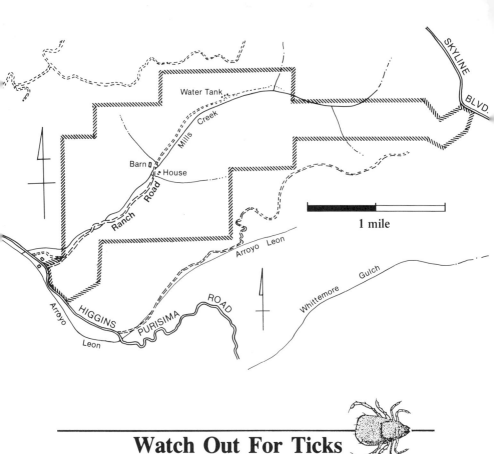

Watch Out For Ticks

  The most dangerous wild animal in the Santa Cruz Mountains is the tick.

  These small blood-sucking arachnids wait on leaves and branches for victims to pass by. Once on board they excavate a hole in the skin and then excrete a powerful cement surrounding their mouthparts. There is about a 4 percent chance that the tick that bites you will be carrying Lyme disease, which is first detected by a circular red rash with a clear center that slowly expands. Later symptoms include fever, joint and muscle pain, fatigue, nausea, and headaches. This disease is most easily treated in its early stages.

BEFORE AN OUTING: *Wear snug-fitting clothes and apply insect repellent containing DEET, especially at the cuffs, neck, and waist.*

AFTER AN OUTING: *Inspect your body thoroughly. If you find a tick grab it with tweezers as close to the skin surface as possible and pull outward with steady, even pressure. Then disinfect the bite with isopropyl alcohol and wash hands with soap and water.*

Butano State Park

TO GET THERE . . . take Cloverdale Road about 3 miles east of Highway 1. The park is about 5 miles south of Pescadero.

It is hard to overstate the charm of this cool, green canyon park. It has a magical rain forest garden of redwoods and ferns cupped between steep ridges, which can be climbed for sweeping vistas.

The easiest hike in the park is on the Creek Trail which can be started on the left side of the road just before reaching the campfire center. This trail is short and mostly level and follows the heavily forested creek bed. More strenuous paths take hikers to the Olmo Fire Trail on the south ridge and the Butano Fire Trail on the north ridge. The Ano Nuevo Trail, stemming from the Olmo Trail, offers a view of Ano Nuevo Island and the ocean on clear days.

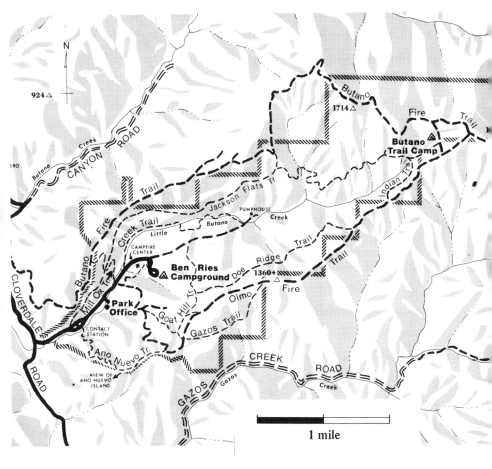

Serious backpackers should consider hiking the ridgetop loop trail to Butano Trailcamp, which can be reached by following the Doe Ridge Trail up a gradual grade to the Olmo Fire Road. Then turn left on the Indian Trail and head about 200 yards to the Fire Road near the trailcamp. The Butano Fire Trail continues to the Jackson Flats Trail which returns to the park entrance area. This hike is about 5.5 miles each way and involves some vigorous hill climbing and a gain of about 1,400 feet to the trailcamp. Enthusiastic hikers may want to make a day of it and hike the loop in one day. Be sure to make reservations in advance to use the camp from May to October by calling park headquarters.

A few miles can be lopped off the loop by continuing on the Indian Trail into the canyon and on to the Jackson Flats Trail.

Hikers with truly extraordinary enthusiasm may want to consider continuing on the Olmo Fire Trail all the way to Big Basin. The legality of hiking this route is still in doubt and camping is not permitted along the way.

Butano State Park is a 2,200 acre enclave of redwoods in the coastal fog belt on the west side of the range. One of its joys is the absence of crowds. Because of its out of the way location you can often walk for hours without passing another hiker.

The Indians usually avoided the shady groves for both practical and religious reasons. They felt the same life force that many hikers still experience today, and were convinced that redwoods were haunted by powerful spirits. That wasn't the only reason they had to stay away, though. The main reason was that edible plants, for both man and deer, are rare in the redwood groves, and the Indians found happier hunting grounds elsewhere. You will notice, however, that redwood forest creekbeds usually have no shortage of banana slugs, salamanders, and newts, and that in addition to steller jays you are likely to see Pygmy nuthatches, chestnut-backed chikadees, winter wrens, and golden-crowned kinglets flying overhead.

In addition to the trailcamp there is also a walk-in campground for car campers. For camping reservations and information call park headquarters at (415) 879-0173.

Calero Reservoir County Park

TO GET THERE... from Highway 101 take Bailey Ave. southwest to McKean Road. Turn right for reservoir access; turn left for trail access and park at the entrance to Calero Farm.

This is one of the noisiest and quietest places in the Santa Cruz Mountains. The reservoir itself is noisy with urban refugees on summer weekends when the lake water is warm and inviting. Powerboats roar with pleasure, and this may seem the last place to find a little solitude.

A quick study of the map, however, reveals that most of this 2,284-acre park lies south of the reservoir and that a large area is now being enjoyed almost exclusively by equestrians and cows.

From Bailey, drive south on McKean a little under a mile to the entrance to Calero Farm. At the road that goes to the farm you will notice a wooden gate at the dirt road trail that loops through the park. Turn right on the first intersecting dirt road which passes a small pond and swings down to near the farm and then up and over the ridge. This route intersects the dirt road you started on and takes you back. The total distance is about 4 miles of easy walking. These generous grassy hills are kept trimmed by the persistent effort of grazing cattle, and are studded with park-like displays of oak, bay, and elderberry.

On the dry southeast part of the Santa Cruz range, Calero has a pronounced split personality. From lush and green during the rainy season, to crisp and brown in the dry months, this park is worth visiting all through the year.

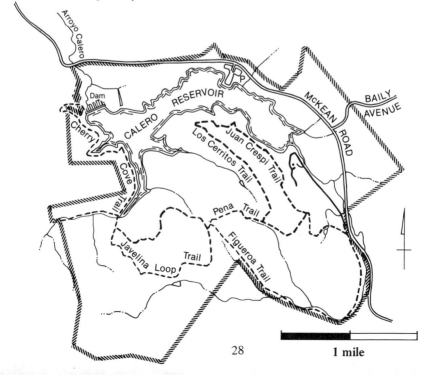

28

1 mile

Cascade Ranch State Park

TO GET THERE. . . . it is along Highway 1 just north and to the east of Año Nuevo State Reserve.

Deep forested canyons, cascading streams, and awesome ridgetop vistas provide a grand setting for the newest state park in the Santa Cruz Mountains.

As of the time this edition goes to press, however, this park is not yet ready for public use. Sensitive ecological and archaeological conditions require that carefully planned trails, parking areas, and other visitor facilities be established before visitors are encouraged.

To get the latest public access information call the state parks office, San Mateo Coast District at (415) 726-6238.

This park is part of the historic 4,088-acre Cascade Ranch, which was saved from becoming a housing development by a coalition of public and private groups under the leadership of the Trust for Public Land, a non-profit organization based in San Francisco.

State legislation preserves about 2,500 acres as a state park; 700 acres for agricultural use with an easement to preclude development; and the remainder to be sold for use as a private campground and a public meeting center. These proposed facilities are still controversial because of their impact on the fragile coastal ecology on the other side of Highway 1.

This park has several well-maintained dirt roads that would make excellent trails. Some abandoned old ranch roads that are overgrown with brush could be cleared and used as foot paths. The dirt road to Chalk Mountain begins among the gentle grassy cow pastures near the ranch buildings and makes a long ascent of the ridge. It climbs through shady forests of Douglas fir and second-growth redwood and onto the dry and rocky ridge where manzanita bush and the hardy knobcone pine abound. This trail goes to the top of Chalk Mountain, in Big Basin

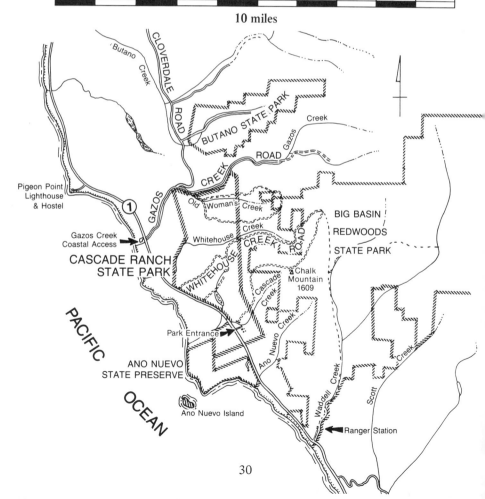

Butano Creek

CLOVERDALE ROAD

BUTANO STATE PARK

GAZOS CREEK ROAD

Gazos Creek

Pigeon Point
Lighthouse
& Hostel

1

GAZOS CREEK ROAD

Old Woman's Creek

BIG BASIN
REDWOODS
STATE PARK

Gazos Creek
Coastal Access

Whitehouse Creek

WHITEHOUSE CREEK ROAD

CASCADE RANCH
STATE PARK

Chalk
Mountain
1609

Cascade Creek

Park Entrance

ANO NUEVO
STATE PRESERVE

Ano Nuevo Creek

Waddell Creek

Scott Creek

PACIFIC

OCEAN

Ano Nuevo Island

Ranger Station

10 miles

State Park, where you will enjoy a 360-degree panorama of the ocean, including Año Nuevo Island, and vast areas of the Santa Cruz Mountains on a clear day. This route intersects Whitehouse Creek Road and passes through a wooded valley on its way back to Cascade Ranch.

With extraordinary diversity of habitat, including coastal scrub, ponds, Douglas fir, freshwater marsh, second-growth redwood, streamside vegetation, and grassland, this area supports an abundance of wildlife. Look for signs of deer, bobcat, coyote, and even mountain lion. Steelhead spawn in Gazos Creek during the rainy season. This is also where Monterey Pine reach the northernmost limit of their natural range.

The Cascade Ranch vicinity is rich in history and prehistory, going back ten thousand years. The Ohlone Indians thrived in this abundant land, feasting on acorns and other edible plants, deer and other game in the mountains, salmon and steelhead in the streams, and mussels, abalone, clams, and other bounty from the sea. Shellmounds attest to many centuries of gourmet dining.

Because of these ideal conditions this place was home to the largest settlement of Ohlone on the coast between Monterey and San Francisco. This is also the place where these Indians first made contact with Spanish explorer Gaspar de Portola during his long trek up the California coast in 1769.

In 1863 Rensselaer and Clara Steele built a 2-story ranch house that is still seen today. It is made of redwood probably milled up the nearby Cascade Creek canyon. From here the Steeles' ran a large dairy farm and later a cheese factory that was famous throughout the state by the end of the nineteenth century.

Call the state park office if you would like to get involved in planning the future of this park.

Barn Owl

Castle Rock State Park

TO GET THERE. . . take Skyline Boulevard about 2.6 miles south from its intersection with Highway 9 (Saratoga Gap).

Spectacular views in all directions, rock outcroppings ideal for climbing, waterfalls, and beautiful groves of oak, madrone, and Douglas fir make this one of my favorite parks.

Castle Rock itself is one of the Bay Area's most popular climbing rocks because of its challenging overhangs and impressive posture on the crest of the range. You can see the ocean and San Francisco Bay from the top. This 80-foot sandstone outcropping, however, is sometimes so congested that climbers must wait their turn to rappel off the summit.

This park covers 3,300 acres and has more than 14 miles of excellent trails. Hiking, picnicking, rock climbing, and backpacking are favorite activities here. To reach some of the outlying areas take the Ridge Trail heading uphill (north) from Saratoga Gap Trail east of the waterfall. Goat Rock, with its formidable south face for climbers, is easily ascended on the uphill side by hikers who marvel at the extraordinary views of Monterey Bay, the Monterey Peninsula, and the Santa Lucia Mountains 80 miles to the south. Continue west on the Ridge Trail for more views and lesser known rocks, and on to Castle Rock Trailcamp.

Exploring "Hole-in-the-Wall" Rock

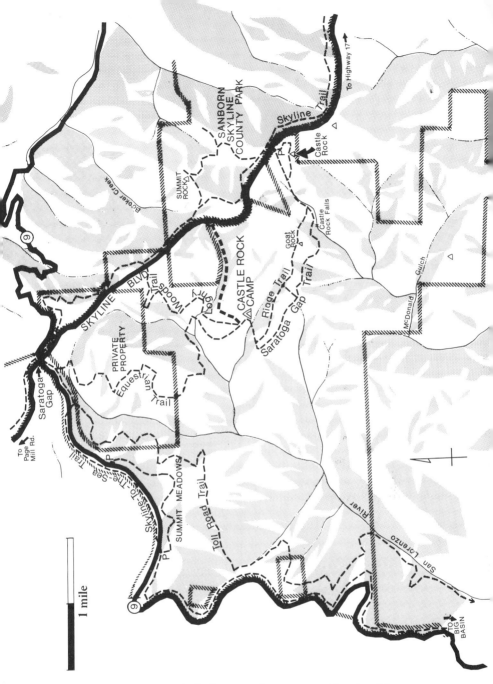

"I am glad I shall never be young without wild
country to be young in."

—Aldo Leopold

Castle Rock is less than half a mile south of the parking lot. The park's main trail, the Saratoga Gap Trail, begins at the opposite end of the parking lot from Skyline and continues through most of the park. About a mile from the parking lot is 100-foot Castle Rock Falls, which can be viewed from an observation platform.

A walk to Castle Rock Trailcamp, about 3.2 miles from the parking lot is a moderate 6.4 mile loop via the Ridge and Saratoga Gap trails. A shorter version of this loop can be made by taking the connecting trail between these two routes.

The Saratoga Gap Trail is on the west slope of the ridge, offering a wonderful chance to see the role of topography on mountain ecology. Compare the deep green of the moist evergreen valleys with the drought-resistant vegetation of the dry and rocky west and south facing ridge-tops. Some of the most beautiful oak, madrone, and chaparral in the Santa Cruz Mountains are in this park.

From the trailcamp the trail heads north to Saratoga Gap, at the intersection of Highway 9 and Skyline Boulevard. The western part of the park was acquired with the help of the Sempervirens fund (P.O. Box 1141, Los Altos, California 94022), which sells an excellent topo-

Tafoni

The shallow caves and honeycomb texture (called "tafoni") in the sandstone outcroppings of the Santa Cruz Mountains are the result of what geologists call "cavernous weathering", a phenomenon that occurs only in a few places in the world.

First, there has to be outcroppings of sandstone cemented together with calcium carbonate in the form of mineral calcite. Next, the extent of cementation has to be variable, so that some parts of the rock are harder than others. And most importantly, this strange weathering only happens where there is a moderately dry climate with a prolonged dry season.

RAINY SEASON: OCTOBER to MAY

Rainwater with dissolved carbon dioxide seeps into rock

graphic map of this park. With its grassy promontories and Douglas fir, madrone, oak, and plenty of sweeping vistas, the Summit Meadows property may be explored by trail from Highway 9 west of Skyline.

This park has an exceptional abundance and variety of spring wildflowers. The parking lot area is a good place to look for the exotically beautiful spotted coral root, a member of the orchid family that has no green, chlorophyll-producing parts. It absorbs energy from decaying organic material in the soil. Grasslands explode with vibrant displays of mule ear, buttercup, baby blue eyes, larkspur, iris, and many others. Because of its higher elevation you can continue enjoying native flowers here long after they have wilted in lower parks. Chaparral blooms with monkey flower, chaparral pea, ceanothus, pitcher sage, and bush poppy, to mention a few.

Because this park can get hot and dry be sure to carry water. Sturdy footwear will come in handy on the rocky sections of trail.

The park's trailcamp has 25 sites, available on a first-come, first-served basis. Water is available. A ranger told me that it has never been filled to capacity. For more information, call park headquarters at (408) 338-6132.

Heavy winter rains seep into the sandstone along cracks and planes of soft rock. The rain water contains carbon dioxide from the air, which dissolves the calcium carbonate that holds the sandstone grains together. The dry season allows the rock to dry out, and the calcium carbonate is then drawn to the surface by the capillary action of water. As the water evaporates, the calcium carbonate is left within a few feet of the surface to form a hard shield that resists erosion. The interior of the rock, however, is left without much cement and easily crumbles away and is removed by water, wind, and animal activity, including people.

Look for spheres of hard rock in the sandstone. These concretions are masses of complete rather than partial cementation. The reddish-brown color is the result of small amounts of iron oxide.

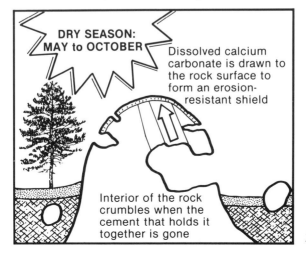

DRY SEASON: MAY to OCTOBER

Dissolved calcium carbonate is drawn to the rock surface to form an erosion-resistant shield

Interior of the rock crumbles when the cement that holds it together is gone

Coal Creek Open Space

TO GET THERE. . . park at the vista point on Skyline Boulevard 1.1 miles north of Page Mill Road and walk down the road that intersects Skyline just to the north. Another access is at the intersection of Skyline and Crazy Pete's Road, 1.8 miles north of Page Mill Road. To visit the Mount Melville area, park on Skyline just north of where it intersects Langley Hill Quarry Road.

This 386-acre preserve slopes eastward from Skyline Boulevard to form a pleasant place to ramble on about 4 miles of ranch roads. As of this writing, however, preserve boundaries and trails are not clearly identified. Be aware that it is easy to get lost if you are not careful.

A pleasant 2.6-mile loop can be taken from the Vista point on Skyline down to Alpine Road to the northeast, where it intersects Crazy Pete's Road and then climbs back to Skyline. On the Crazy Pete's Road trail, just uphill from Alpine Road, a footbridge crosses a beautiful cascading series of waterfalls that is particularly impressive during the rainy season. The area is covered with oak, bay, some very large madrone, and grasslands. A clear day will reveal some great views of the south Bay Area.

The easy walk up Mount Melville, southwest of where Skyline Boulevard intersects Langley Hill Quarry Road, is rewarded by spectacular views of the Santa Cruz Mountains vicinity, stretching well out to sea to the west and to the bay and beyond to the east. Most of the hill is open grassland, but at the top is a stately grove of oak, bay, and madrone that offers shelter from the wind and sun.

For more information contact the Midpeninsula Regional Open Space District at (415) 949-5500.

SEE MAP ON PAGE 90

Duveneck Windmill Pasture Area

TO GET THERE. . . take Moody Road west past Foothill College in Los Altos Hills, and turn left on Rhus Ridge Road. Park at the gate near a tennis court.

Rising through the foothills of the Santa Cruz Mountains and up the steep Monte Bello Ridge, this 761-acre park has close urban proximity for casual day walks and access to adjoining parks for more strenuous outings.

From the gate, hike the short but steep dirt road to the top of the ridge. This stretch of trail is strenuous, but the rewards are great and the grade levels out when you reach the ridgetop, with wonderful panoramas of the hills and mountains to the west, including Black Mountain. At the top of the ridge the trail forks in 3 directions. Take the middle route, which heads west through the oak-studded grasslands and then swings south for a view of an old metal windmill in a grassy clearing.

A vigorous and spectacular 3.5 mile trail to the top of Black Mountain, in Monte Bello Open Space, makes an exciting and invigorating event. The trail goes through private property part of the way, so call Hidden Villa Ranch for permission: (415) 948-4690. By arranging a car shuttle you can walk about 7 scenic and inspiring miles from Windmill Pasture, up Black Mountain, and north on Monte Bello Ridge to Page Mill Road. A trailcamp near Black Mountain allows the trip to be broken into two days and allows the rare opportunity to spend a night in the grasslands east of Skyline.

The Windmill Pasture was part of the 2,300-acre Hidden Villa Ranch, which was owned by Frank and Josephine Duveneck between 1923 and 1977, when they gave it to the public as a preserve. The windmill is a remnant of the generations of ranching in these hills. Just west of the preserve is Hidden Villa Ranch, famous for its Youth Hostel and environmental education programs.

Though it is not geographically connected, this park is classified as part of the Rancho San Antonio Open Space Preserve. For further information, call the Midpeninsula Regional Open Space district at (415) 965-4717.

If you get a chance to observe scrub jays in action you might notice that they are Nature's tree planters. Scrub jays are busy little fellows who often bury acorns in the ground, and then get sidetracked by other important duties and forget where the treasure was left. They win whether they remember or not, though , since they can either eat the acorns or let them grow into oak trees for the benefit of future generations of scrub jays.

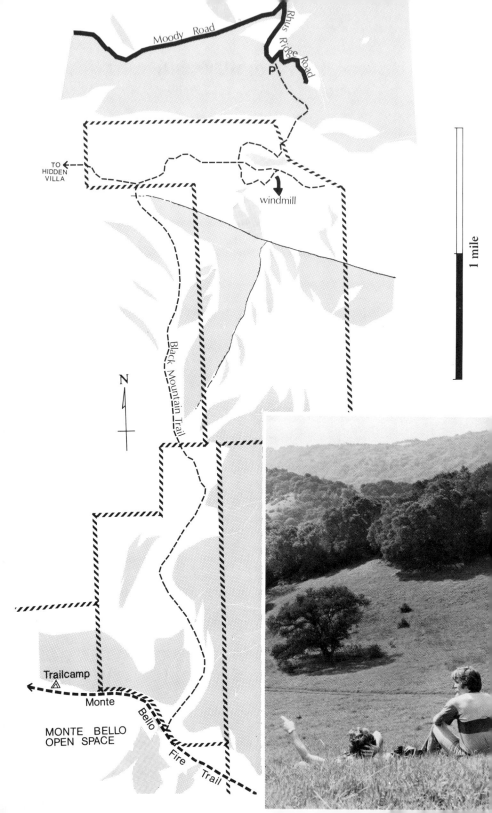

Moody Road

Rhus Ridge Road

P

TO
HIDDEN
VILLA

windmill

1 mile

N

Black Mountain Trail

Trailcamp

Monte

Bello

MONTE BELLO
OPEN SPACE

Fire

Trail

Duveneck Windmill Pastures was donated to the Midpeninsula Regional Open Space District by Frank and Josephine Duveneck. The 1800 acres next to the preserve is Hidden Villa Ranch, which was purchased by the Duvenecks in the mid-1920's and is operated as a working farm. At the same time they opened their land to the outside world by establishing a youth hostel, helping to found the Loma Prieta chapter of the Sierra Club, and by starting environmental education programs for children.

The ranch is now protected in perpetuity by Hidden Villa Inc., a non-profit organization. If you are interested in more information about activities and ways to help, contact Hidden Villa Inc., 26870 Moody Road, Los Altos Hills, CA 94022; or phone (415) 948-4690 for office and farm tours; (415) 941-6407 for hostel and camp; and (415) 941-6119 for environmental projects.

Acorn Woodpeckers

When you see a dead tree trunk or branch riddled with holes and stocked with acorns then you have made yourself a guest in the territory of a colony of woodpeckers.

These raucous birds fill the air with a shrill "JACK-A jack-a" and are easily identified in flight by flashes of black and white on their wings and a glimmering red crown.

This is one of the few species of colonial woodpeckers, with all members of the community tending the eggs and young and digging out nesting holes in trees.

The most interesting time to watch these birds is in September and October when they gather acorns for winter provisions and wedge them tightly into holes in trees, fence posts, and even telephone poles so that squirrels can't pry them out. With binoculars you can easily see woodpeckers position the acorns pointed-end first into holes, and then lodge them in securely with a few good whacks with their beaks.

The endangered Bay Checkerspot Butterfly is protecting Edgewood from a proposed golf course.

Edgewood County Park

TO GET THERE . . . the main entrance is on Edgewood Road at Old Stagecoach Road opposite Crestview Drive. Other accesses are at Edgewood Road just west of Highway 280 where a trail goes under the freeway and into the park; and at the intersection of Hillcrest Way and Sunset in Redwood City.

The grasslands of this 467-acre park are famous for some of the Bay Area's most spectacular displays of springtime wildflowers. Because of its easy access to the Redwood City area, this is a wonderful place for picnics and short walks that take only a few hours out of the day.

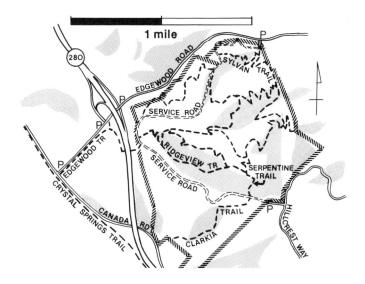

Edgewood has clearly-marked trails, popular with walkers and equestrians, that climb the forested 800-foot ridge in the center of the park and circle the grassland perimeter.

The park's serpentine grasslands support 7 rare and endangered plant species and the endangered Bay Checkerspot Butterfly. Serpentine, associated with fault zones, provides poor soil for non-native plants because of its high toxicity and low water-holding capacity, but encourages the growth of indigenous flowering plants in great abundance. In April look for dazzling displays of goldfields, blue-eyed grass, tidy tips, and buttercups, to name a few.

As of this writing the future of this park is still in doubt. The San Mateo County Board of Supervisors has voted to build a golf course that would destroy most of the serpentine grasslands. Your support for saving Edgewood is needed.

The county has added a 150-person youth day camp.

Santa Cruz Mountains Geology

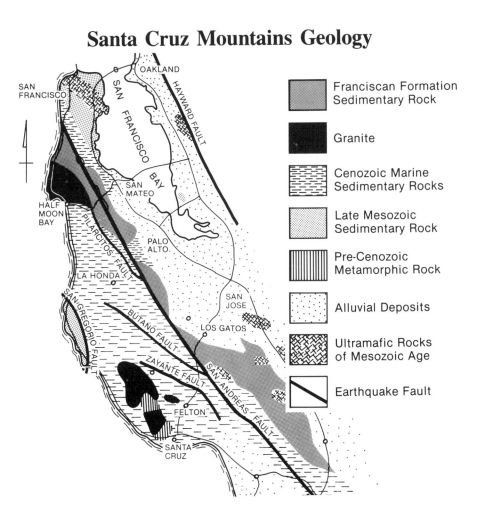

El Corte de Madera Creek Open Space

TO GET THERE. . . from Highway 92 take Skyline Boulevard south 8.6 miles to the Caltrans Rest Stop at Skegg's Point. It is 3.9 miles north of Woodside Road. From Skegg's Point walk north about a quarter of a mile to where two roads intersect at Skyline and take the dirt road to the right. There is another access half a mile south of Skegg's Point, across from the Methuselah Tree.

At the headwaters of El Corte de Madera Creek, this 2,789-acre preserve combines scenic ridgetops and ocean views with deep verdant valleys filled with second-growth redwood and Douglas fir.

This preserve's most popular attraction is a spectacular sandstone formation with shallow caves and honeycomb depressions reminiscent of outcroppings at Castle Rock State Park, though it seems to be made of a softer and more fragile material. For this reason climbing is not allowed. You will find a description of how these features were formed in the Castle Rock chapter.

Some spectacular views are revealed along the ridgetop near the rock, especially at Vista Point, where low brush allows a good panorama to the south and west, stretching way out to sea on a clear day. This is a fine place for a lunch break, wind and fog permitting.

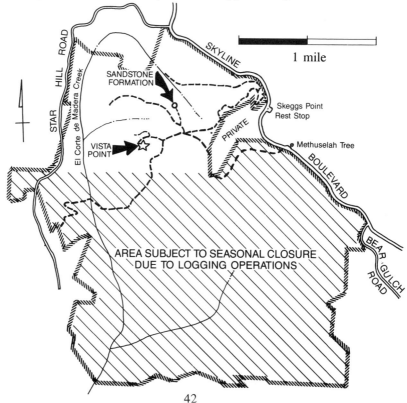

42

All of the trails here are old logging roads, some of which will continue to be used to haul out timber through 1989 in accordance with the terms of purchase. For your safety please contact the open space district before visiting prior to 1990. As of this writing none of these trails are marked, making it easy to get lost.

For more information and a current trail map call the Midpeninsula Regional Open Space District at (415) 949-5500.

El Sereno Open Space

TO GET THERE... from Highway 17 take Montevina Road 3 miles west to its end where a turnout provides parking for a few cars.

This 1,068-acre preserve spans 2 miles of scenic ridgetop and steep canyons on the east side of the range. Chaparral covers most of the area, with oak, madrone, and bay scattered through the area, providing islands of shade for summer visitors. Beautiful groves of madrone and bay grow on the north and east sides of the ridge.

A good time to visit is in early spring, when chamise, ceanothus and other chaparral vegetation burst forth with new growth and are adorned with an abundance of flowers. Use your nose often here to appreciate the spicy aromas that offer a special appeal in this kind of plant community. You will see and hear lots of birds as they feed off the many seeds and berries that grow here.

Another advantage of chaparral is that it is low enough that it doesn't obstruct the commanding vistas of the Santa Cruz Mountains and the urbanized Santa Clara Valley. To the north you will see Black Mountain, Oakland, and even Mount Tamalpais, and to the southeast stands Mount Umunhum. The views are particularly stunning on those cold, crystal clear days of winter when the smog and haze are gone from the valley below.

Most of the trails through this park are dirt roads, and if you have ever tried cross-country hiking through chaparral you will appreciate why this is a good place for sticking to the established trails. Hikers should also be aware that this is one of the region's driest parks and water should be carried. Animals you might see here include woodrats, black-tail deer, rabbits, and coyotes.

This park is open for day use only. For more information, call the Midpeninsula Regional Open Space District at (415) 965-4717.

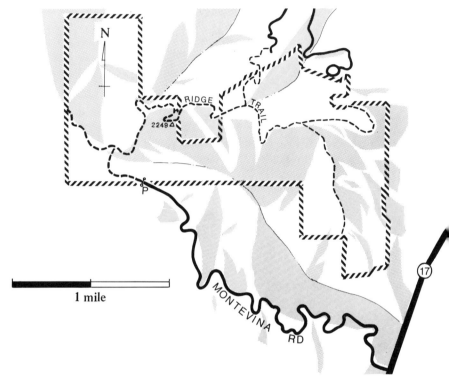

Foothills Open Space

TO GET THERE. . . it is on the south side of Page Mill Road, about a mile uphill from the entrance to Foothills Park. Enter at a brown metal gate.

This small preserve is covered mainly with chaparral and oak. From the Page Mill Road entrance an easy half-mile trail goes to a rounded grassy knoll with a wide view of the southern Bay Area. A very steep trail continues on down to Hidden Villa Ranch.

This is one of the open space preserves where dog walking is allowed. Be sure to keep your pet on a leash.

Because of limited parking you are encouraged to call the Mid-peninsula Regional Open Space District at (415) 949-5500 before visiting.

Where to Walk Your Dog

Dogs are not welcome on most trails in the Santa Cruz Mountains. Being natural predators they love to chase deer and rabbits; and even leashed canines can terrorize wildlife with their carnivore scent.

Policies concerning dogs:

Midpeninsula Regional Open Space Preserves: *Leashed dogs are allowed in designated portions of the following preserves:*

- *Foothills Open Space.*
- *Fremont Older Open Space.*
- *Long Ridge Open Space, at the grassy area at the Grizzly Flat entrance.*
- *Windy Hill Open Space.*

Look for signs identifying where dog walking is allowed.

State Beaches: *Dogs are allowed at state beaches on the Santa Cruz Mountains coast except at Half Moon Bay and Año Nuevo.*

State Parks: *Dogs are prohibited on park trails. They are allowed on leash at parking lots, campsites, and along paved roads.*

Santa Clara County Parks: *Dogs are not allowed on trails, but may be taken on leash to road access parts of the following parks:*

- *Almaden Quicksilver: Senator Mine area.*
- *Lexington Reservoir.*
- *Mount Madonna: Valley View campground #1 and day use area.*
- *Sanborn-Skyline: Picnic areas.*
- *Santa Teresa: All road access sites except golf course.*
- *Stevens Creek: Picnic areas.*
- *Uvas Canyon.*

San Mateo County Parks: *Dogs are not permitted.*

Foothill Park

TO GET THERE. . . take Page Mill Road in Palo Alto west of Highway 280.

The city of Palo Alto operates a 1,400 acre "nature preserve" in the low foothills west of town. The park, on the steep eastern slopes of the Santa Cruz Mountains, is characterized by grasslands, chaparral, oak, madrone, bay, buckeye, and a big lawn and picnic area. You may also appreciate the small reservoir for fishing near the park entrance and the nature interpretive center, near the lawn, that has an educational exhibit of native plants and animals.

These wide, grassy expanses are inhabited by multitudes of ground squirrels and the birds of prey which feed on them. Many species of birds are easily seen here — so bring binoculars.

The park changes from season to season and is pleasant for hiking all year, though my favorite time is the green, flowering months of early spring. The preserve has about 15 miles of hiking trails, including several scenic loops of 5 to 7 miles, with some nice vistas of the south Bay Area.

Unfortunately for most Bay Area hikers this park is open only to Palo Alto residents and their guests, and you will be asked for identification at the gate. For information about the regularly scheduled nature walks, call park headquarters at (415) 329-2423.

The park is open for day use only.

Coyote

The Forest of Nisene Marks State Park

TO GET THERE... take the Aptos Creek Road north from Soquel Drive in Aptos.

The Forest of Nisene Marks is a vast and rugged semi-wilderness, with few of the facilities we normally expect from state parks. It's a diverse land of redwood forests, riperian woodlands, oak groves, stands of knobcone pine, and chaparral; and it has a robust pioneer history whose remnants are rotting away and becoming part of the landscape.

This park has few camping and picnicking facilities, but it has lots of hiking trails and some beautiful forest scenery. Some of these trails, however, being poorly marked, may be hard to follow and should be taken cautiously to avoid getting lost in this dense coastal redwood forest. Camping is permitted only at the trailcamp near the Sand Point Overlook, a 6 mile hike from the Aptos Creek Road trailhead by way of West Ridge Trail. It can also be reached by hiking 5.4 miles on Buzzard Lagoon Road and the Aptos Fire road past the locked gate off Eureka Canyon Road.

This forest was a source of Bay Area Lumber between 1870 and 1925 and few first-growth redwoods now remain; but some of the remnants of the lumber industry can still be found on the Loma Prieta Grade Trail, which follows an old railroad bed. Three miles from the trailhead is Hoffman's Historic Site (formerly China Camp), consisting of a few deteriorating wooden buildings and bridges dating back to the lumber boom years.

The Loma Prieta Grade and West Ridge trails wind through some steep terrain and can be strenuous for beginners; but the entire loop is only about 7 miles and at an easy pace almost anyone should be able to make it. You can hike north on the West Ridge Trail to the trailcamp. Watch out for poison oak in this area.

A strenuous loop hike of more than 19 miles, and a gain of more

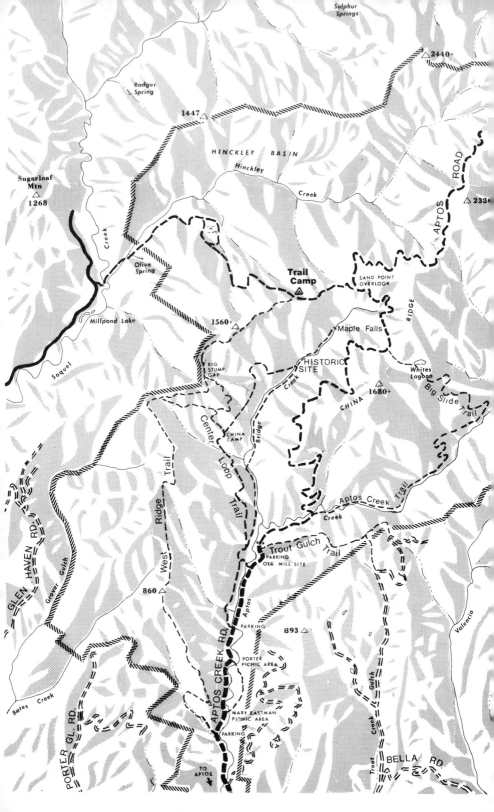

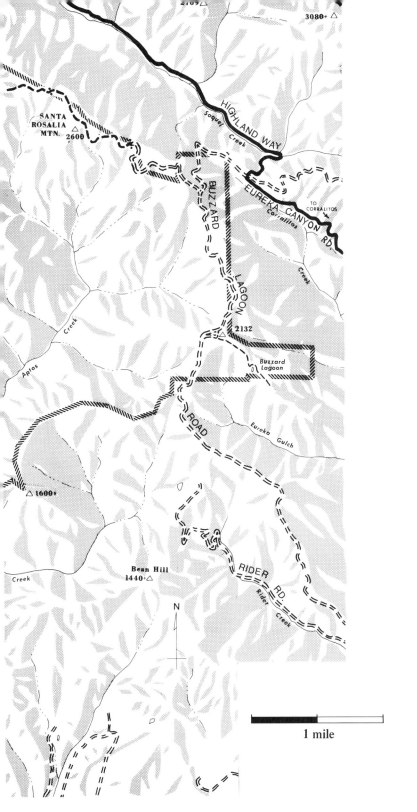

SANTA
ROSALIA
MTN. 2600

HIGHLAND WAY

Soquel Creek

EUREKA CANYON RD.

TO
CORRALITOS

Corralitos

BUZZARD

3080+

Creek

2132

LAGOON

Buzzard
Lagoon

Creek

Eureka Gulch

Aptos

ROAD

1600+

Creek

RIDER RD.

Bean Hill
1440+

Rider Creek

N

1 mile

than 1,000 feet, can be achieved by combining the Aptos Creek Fire Road with West Ridge Trail and Loma Prieta Grade. Despite the long uphill grade, the Aptos Creek Fire Road will reward you with views of the surrounding mountains and occasionally the ocean. Fossil seashells are common in the exposed road cuts as this route climbs above the redwoods and into oak, madrone, and chaparral.

Except for the strident call of steller jays, there is often a profound sense of quiet that contributes to the cathedral qualities of the redwood groves. The tall trees let little light reach the ground, and their thick, soft bark seems to actually absorb sound and light, creating a mood of sober tranquility. I know of no other trees which can have such a profound and immediate influence on a hiker's mood. It takes only a few of the trees in a grove to create a feeling of dark dignity and quiet.

The park covers nearly 10,000 acres and all the creeks that flow through it originate within its boundaries. These brawling arteries of life support their own plant communities and have vertical gardens of five finger ferns hanging from their moist, shady banks.

Mountain Lions sometimes sneak through the park, though they are rarely seen. Look for their paw prints beside mud puddles after rains or along creek beds.

The park is open daily from 6 a.m. until sunset. Horses and firearms are not allowed, and ground fires are prohibited at the trailcamp. There are 2 picnic areas, both along Aptos Creek Road.

For further information and trailcamp reservations, call (408) 335-4598 or write: Henry Cowell Redwoods State Park, P.O. Box P-1, Felton, California 95018.

Fremont Older Open Space

TO GET THERE... from Saratoga-Sunnyvale Road, take Prospect Road west to the end of the road. A trail into the park can also be taken from the Villa Maria area of Stevens Creek County Park off Stevens Canyon Road.

This 734-acre preserve near Cupertino is a low and easy land of gentle hills and leisurely walks. The 4.5 miles of trails ramble through oakwoods, grasslands, chaparral, hayfields, and remnant walnut and apricot groves that still bear fruit. Since 1870 this land has produced grapes, apricots, prunes, walnuts, and olives.

This park is a gentle blend of natural and agricultural qualities; but it still hosts a wonderful abundance of wildlife. Deer roam freely, squirrels trapeze across the green leafy forest canopy, and woodpeckers tap holes in oak trees. I also discovered that rattlesnakes make their home here. Bounding down a steep hill I heard a rattling sound that let me know that I was getting too close to a disgruntled snake. I leaped to a respectable distance from the startled serpent and watched him glide into the bushes. Despite a bad reputation, they are actually good natured fellows who usually try to avoid trouble — and they even sound a warning when people get too close.

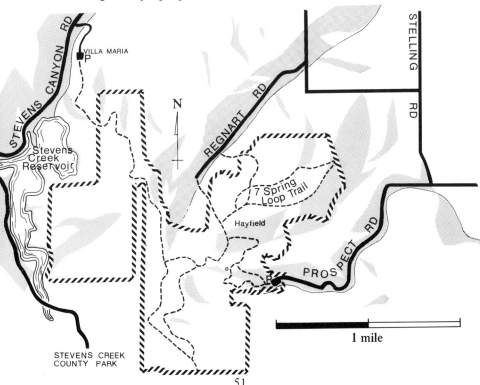

The home of distinguished San Francisco newspaper editor Fremont Older, which was originally built in 1911, has been faithfully restored and is open to the public occasionally for group tours. The property was purchased by the Midpeninsula Regional Open Space District in 1975, and the house is under private lease.

The park is open from dawn to dusk and fire arms and motor vehicles are prohibited. Be sure to carry water, especially during the summer months. Most of the park's trails are dirt ranch roads. For more information, call the Midpeninsula Regional Open Space District at (415) 965-4717.

Dogs on leashes are allowed in designated areas.

Poison Oak

The bad news is that poison oak is common in the Santa Cruz Mountains. But the good news is that it can be easily identified and the ill effects can normally only be acquired by physical contact with the plant. The only exception is by inhaling its smoke or by touching objects, pets, or people who have rubbed against it.

Fortunately for the 70 percent of the population that is at least mildly sensitive to the urushiol oil found in this shrub, contact is easily avoided. The Santa Cruz Mountains have many broad trails, including former ranch and logging roads, where you will be able to keep a safe distance.

If you do accidentally rub against poison oak leaves or stems (in winter some plants lack identifying leaves), a washing with soap and warm water will reduce the severity of the rash if done soon after contact.

Golden Gate National Recreation Area

SWEENEY RIDGE

TO GET THERE . . . from Highway 280 in San Bruno, take Sneath Lane west to a locked gate. The road continues as a trail. The park is also accessible from the south side of Skyline College, which is at the end of College Drive, off Skyline Boulevard in San Bruno. A dirt road runs south from the college to Sweeney Ridge.

This is a place to go for breathtaking Bay Area views and spring wildflowers. On a clear day you can see the Pacific Ocean, the Farallon Islands, Mount Tamalpais, San Bruno Mountain, Mount Diablo, San Francisco Bay, Mount Hamilton, Moffett Field, San Andreas Lake, and many cities ringing the bay. This is a good place to become familiar with Bay Area geography.

Of course, these spectacular views can only be seen on clear days; and when the ridge is shrouded in ocean fog walkers can easily become disoriented, and even lost.

From the gate on Sneath Lane, the trail climbs about 600 feet and 1.9 miles to the Portola Discovery Site at an elevation of 1280 feet. The road itself is on national park land, but both sides are in the San Francisco watershed, where public access is prohibited. The actual discovery site is on a small parcel of land that is still owned by San Mateo County, and is marked by 2 stone monuments, one to Portola, and another dedicated to the late conservationist Carl McCarthy.

At this place, on November 4, 1769, Captain Gaspar de Portola, seeking Monterey Bay, accidentally found the large arm of the ocean which was named San Francisco Bay. Portola thought that this inland sea was Drakes Bay, near Point Reyes, and was disappointed to have missed Monterey Bay. After returning to San Diego he realized that

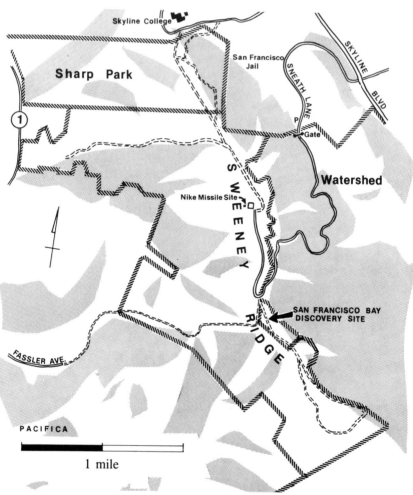

this bay, one of the world's best natural harbors, was a new discovery and a perfect place for a Spanish presidio.

Covering 1047 acres, Sweeney Ridge is covered mostly with coastal scrub and grasses. Wildflowers are abundant in April and May, including checkermallow, Indian paintbrush, lupine, colombine, and blue-eyed grass. This is also an excellent place to see a wide variety of birds.

From near the discovery site, the Sneath Lane trail veers sharply north and ends at an abandoned Nike missile site. From here, a dirt road continues north and downhill to Sharp Park and Skyline College. South from the discovery site a dirt road traces the ridgetop to the boundary with the watershed property, which is off limits to hikers.

The struggle to save Sweeney Ridge is a case history in grassroots conservation. It started when Pacificans United to Save Our Hills

(PUSH) submitted 5,000 signatures to Congressman Leo Ryan, who then requested a national park study. When Ryan was murdered in Guyana, Congressman Phillip Burton, who has been called the father of the Golden Gate National Recreation Area, introduced a bill to include Sweeney Ridge in the G.G.N.R.A. Meanwhile the Trust for Public Land delayed plans to develop the ridge by purchasing a 3-year option to buy it.

Burton pushed the bill through, but Secretary of the Interior James Watt refused to permit the National Park Service to buy the land. When Watt resigned, the new Interior Secretary William Clark, with encouragement from Representatives Sala Burton, Pete McCloskey, and Tom Lantos, and both California senators, went ahead with the purchase.

The National Park Service offers ranger-guided walks on Saturdays dealing with natural and human history. Rangers also lead walks from Fassler Avenue in Pacifica. As of this writing this route passes through private property and is only accessible with ranger escort. For more information, call (415) 556-8642 or (415) 556-8371.

Sweeney Ridge is often foggy, and usually windy, especially in the afternoon; so dress appropriately.

FORT FUNSTON

TO GET THERE... from Highway 280 take John Daly Boulevard west and turn north on Skyline Boulevard (Highway 35). It's in the southwest corner of San Francisco, just west of Lake Merced.

The hills of San Francisco are actually the northernmost foothills of the Santa Cruz Mountains. At Fort Funston you can see the only part of this city that is still anything close to its natural condition.

Covered with sand dunes, as most of western San Francisco was

originally, this 116-acre area was spared from development by the army in the early 1900's. Named for General Frederick Funston, a hero of the Spanish-American War, the fort was established to help defend the coast against foreign invasion.

The strategic value of the fort was updated during World War I and World War II with the latest artillery, and afterwards as a Nike missile base.

Fort Funston is ideal for easy walks and for exploring relics of military history. It also has a wheelchair-accessible paved trail. Be sure to watch for hang gliders soaring along the bluffs above the beach.

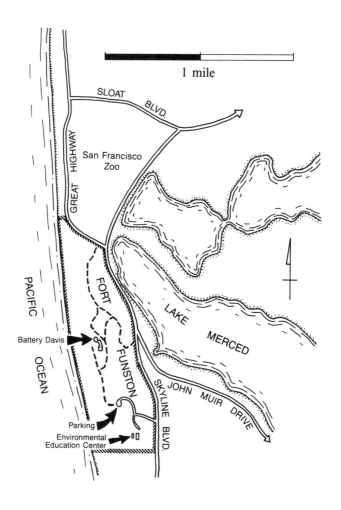

Hassler Open Space

TO GET THERE. . . from Interstate 280 take Edgewood Road east, turn left on Crestview Road, and left on Edmonds Road. Park across from Redwood Center on Edmonds Road and walk up Hassler Road to a gate which marks the preserve boundary.

This 293-acre preserve covers a ridge and 2 wooded valleys in the dry eastern foothills of the Santa Cruz Mountains. Named for the Hassler Health Home, a tuberculosis sanitarium which operated here from 1926 to 1972, the land is now in the process of reverting to a more natural condition. Relics of its former use still abound, though, with abandoned fire hydrants and steps that go nowhere.

The hills are covered mainly with a combination of oak groves, chaparral, and grasslands. There are also a variety of ornamental trees and shrubs, especially around the site of the sanitarium, that seem to have adapted to our summer drought cycle.

There are no real trails here, as of this writing, except for the rapidly deteriorating Hassler Road, which leads to the ridge top. Because the section of Hassler Road between Redwood Center and the gate is private, be sure to stay on the road in this area.

For more information, contact the Midpeninsula Regional Open Space District at (415) 949-5500.

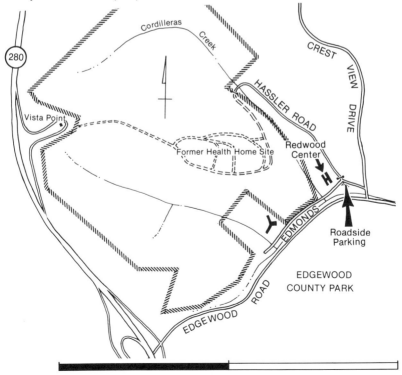

1 mile

Henry Cowell Redwoods State Park

TO GET THERE... The southern unit is just south of Felton on Highway 9. The Fall Creek unit is just northwest of town on the Felton-Empire Road.

This redwood-forested park is divided into 2 sizable units in the mountains near Felton.

Most visitors are unaware that the popular Redwood Grove and picnic area just south of Felton are only a small part of the park. The great bulk of the southern unit of this redwood preserve can be reached by well developed hiking trails from several roadside pullouts on Highway 9, from the park campground on Graham Hill Road, and from the picnic area near park headquarters (the day use entrance). This unit covers 1,737 acres and has about 15 miles of hiking trails.

The Redwood Grove nature trail loop (near the picnic area) is the easiest and most popular trail in the park. It is less than 1 mile and

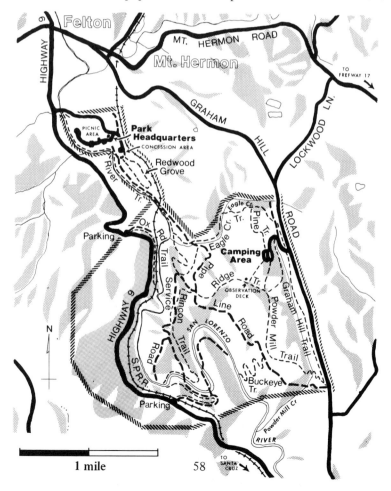

is more of a stroll than a real hike, though it winds through one of the finest first-growth redwood groves south of San Francisco, and is especially pleasant on weekdays when the crowds are gone. Most of the redwoods in the rest of the park are second-growth.

This is a hilly park, and the vegetation corresponds to the area's geography. Lower areas are forested with redwood and riperian vegetation in places, and ridges and hilltops are covered with oak, madrone, digger pine, manzanita, and other chaparral plants. The distribution of plants is also connected to the availability of sunlight. Chaparral plants prefer the sunny ridgetops, while the understory plants of the redwood groves are satisfied with only indirect light and with occasional shafts of sunlight that penetrate the dense forest canopy.

A cross section of the park's ecology can be viewed on a short hike from the picnic area to the observation deck on the Ridge Trail, which climbs from the redwood-covered streambeds to the chaparral-covered ridgetops where a view of Santa Cruz and Monterey Bay are possible on clear days. The route is steep in places and there is little water along most of the trail, especially in summer. The trail, however, is only slightly more than 3 miles and is easily completed in 2 hours by most hikers. The observation deck, on the water tank at the highest point of the trail, is a good place to relax and eat lunch.

The Fall Creek Unit

The Fall Creek unit is a steep, forested, and completely magnificent 2,335 acre park, tucked into a rugged canyon northwest of Felton. Start from the parking lot just off Felton-Empire Road and hike upstream. Where the north and south forks of Fall Creek meet, follow the

Take the leisurely walk to the old lime kilns.

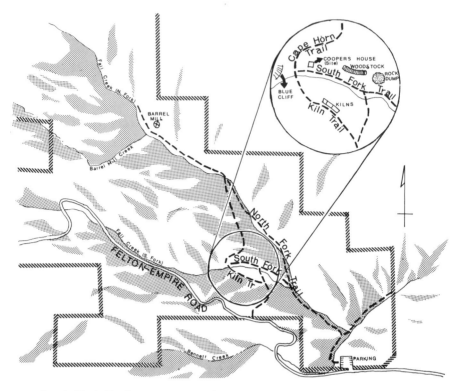

South Fork Trail upstream to a flat area in a beautiful grove of maples, which becomes a brilliant blaze of color in autumn.

Most of this deep and shady canyon is occupied by second-growth redwoods, along with bay, big-leaf maple, and douglas fir. The forest floor is carpeted with sorrel, wild ginger, several kinds of ferns, and Solomon's seal, and chaparral grows on a few dry places.

Here the IXL Lime Company built 3 lime kilns in 1870, which were fired with split redwood logs, some of which are still stacked across the creek from the kilns. By 1880 this was one of the state's most important lime producers. Above these deteriorated kilns rises Blue Cliff, an old limestone quarry.

From the kiln area hike the Cape Horn Trail to the North Fork Trail and follow the creek upstream to the scattered remains of a water-powered barrel mill which was built in 1912. From here hike down-stream and back to the trailhead.

Fall Creek itself is one of the park's most wonderful features. It bounces wild and cold all summer, splashing over granite boulders which make it reminiscent of High Sierra streams. This beautiful canyon has more delightful qualities than I can mention here and is one of my favorite places in the Santa Cruz Mountains.

For more information, call park headquarters at (408) 335-4598.

Huddart County Park

TO GET THERE . . . take **Woodside Road 3.5 miles west from Highway 280 and turn north on Kings Mountain Road.**

This is one of San Mateo County's most popular parks, and its many recreational facilities often make it more crowded than most hikers like. Fortunately, however, you can leave the parking lots and picnic areas behind and explore about 15 miles of trails. The park covers 973 acres of oak woodlands, chaparral, and Douglas fir and redwood forests.

This is a steep park, with trails to match. Easy walkers may want to take the .75 mile nature trail near the park entrance station. A more challenging route follows West Union Creek via Richard's Road Trail to near the Youth Group Camp, and then returns by way of the Service Road. A more ambitious loop around the park, climbing the 2,000 foot Skyline Ridge may be accomplished by continuing uphill on the Richard's Road Trail, turn left on the Skyline Trail, and left (downhill) on the Chinquapin Trail.

This route offers a cross section of Santa Cruz Mountains ecology. Oak woodlands cover the park's lower elevations, with chaparral on dry ridgetops and redwood groves are tucked into streambed furrows. Tanoak, madrone, bay, Douglas fir, and several species of oak also contribute to this plant kingdom hodgepodge. The park's animal inhabitants include Black-tail deer, squirrels, racoons, foxes, bobcats, woodrats, several species of lizards and snakes, and an abundant variety of birds.

The Woodside Store is a nearby historic site worth visiting, built in 1853 by Dr. Orville Tripp. At one time it was within 5 miles of 15 sawmills.

An understanding of the human history of the park is important for an appreciation of what you will see here. The redwood groves you see are second-growth descendants of an ancient forest of giants that was logged in the 1850's and 60's to supply the Bay Area's booming cities with lumber. You can still see massive stump remnants of the original forest and trace the "skid road" depressions up the hillsides, created by oxen dragging logs to the nearby sawmills.

This park has more than the usual recreational opportunties. A childrens' playground, a horse ring, bridle paths, picnicking and barbecuing facilities, and an archery range are provided, and an overnight campground is open in summer on a first-come, first-serve basis.

For more information, call the park at (415) 851-0326.

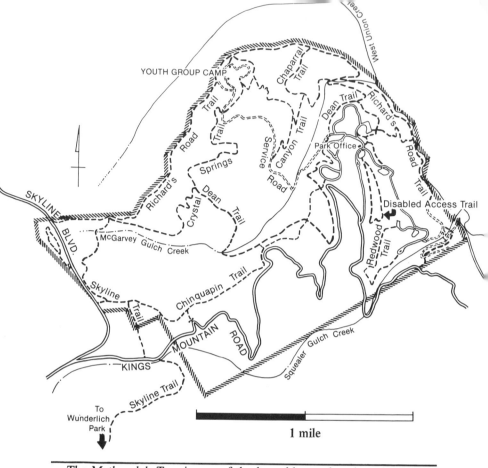

YOUTH GROUP CAMP

West Union Creek

Chaparral Trail

Dean Trail

Richard's Road Trail

Park Office

Trail

Road

Richard's Road

Springs

Service Road

Canyon Trail

Disabled Access Trail

Crystal

Dean Trail

SKYLINE BLVD.

McGarvey Gulch Creek

Redwood Trail

Skyline

Chinquapin Trail

Skyline Trail

MOUNTAIN ROAD

Squealer Gulch Creek

KINGS

Skyline Trail

To Wunderlich Park

1 mile

The Methuselah Tree is one of the last old-growth redwoods along Skyline Boulevard. It's just east of Skyline about half a mile south of Skeggs Point.

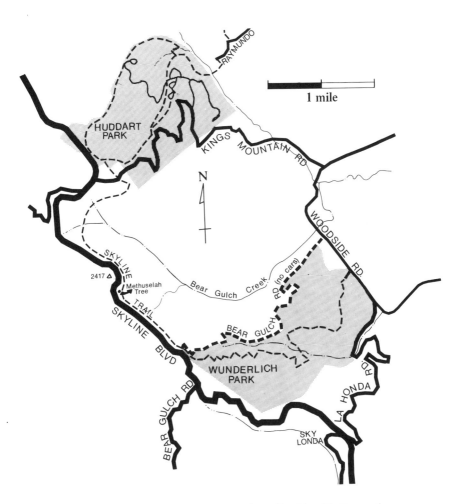

San Mateo County's ongoing Skyline Corridor Trail may be explored from Huddart Park. A scenic ridgetop riding and hiking trail follows Skyline Boulevard for about 5 miles between Huddart and Wunderlich county parks. Passing through the California Water Company's Bear Gulch Watershed, this trail passes near the "Methuselah" redwood. At 15 feet in diameter and estimated to be 1,500 years old, this is one of the few old-growth giants left in this area. A car shuttle between Huddart and Wunderlich will make this trail the key link in a grand all-day excursion.

Jasper Ridge Biological Preserve

HOW TO GET THERE . . . there are two entrances. **To reach the Sears-ville Lake entrance take Sand Hill Road west from Highway 280. To reach the Escobar Gate entrance take Alpine Road west from Highway 280, turn right on Westridge Drive, and right on Escobar Road.**

Jasper Ridge is famous for its spectacular springtime displays of wildflowers and remnants of native California grasslands. Operated by Stanford University, this preserve boasts examples of all of the plant communities found in the Santa Cruz Mountains.

The ridge's serpentine soils, lacking essential nutrients needed by most plants, allow native grasses to resist the invasion of alien annuals. Of the 16 grasses found on the serpentine, 12 are natives, including purple needle grass, pin bluegrass, and big squirreltail. This serpentine community, including the checkerspot butterfly, has been the object of much scientific study of ecology and population biology.

This 1300-acre preserve is only accessible by docent escort. Guided walks are regularly scheduled and independent group tours may be arranged. Docent walks observe wildflowers, birds, geology, lichens, trees, grasses, and other areas of interest. For more information, call Stanford University at (415) 327-2277.

La Honda Creek Open Space

TO GET THERE. . . from Skyline Boulevard take Bear Gulch Road .6 miles west and turn left on Allen Road. The preserve entrance is at a metal gate that crosses the road 1.1 miles from Bear Gulch Road.

PLEASE NOTE: Because Allen Road is private, you must have a permit to enter this preserve. To obtain one, contact the Midpeninsula Regional Open Space District office at (415) 949-5500. Because parking is not allowed outside the main gate, you will get the combination to the gate lock when you receive the permit.

The best thing about this 583-acre preserve is the wonderful variety of scenery revealed by even a short and leisurely walk.

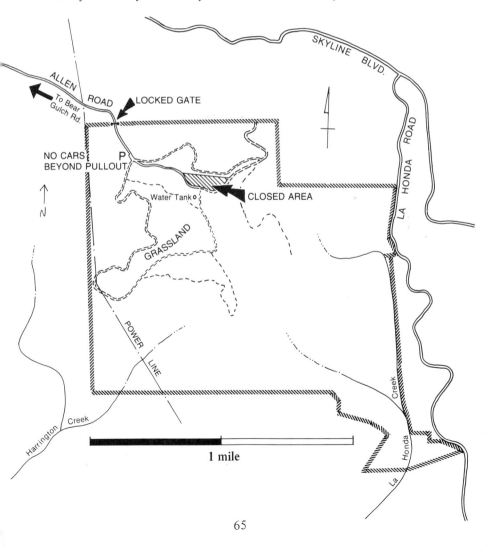

Gentle grassland slopes provide unobstructed mountain and ocean views to the south and west. Oak-madrone woodlands occupy the higher and drier zones, mixing easily with Douglas fir, and then blending quickly with second-growth redwood in the moist and shady canyon bottoms.

Even a 2-to-4 mile ramble will take you through all courses of this ecological smorgasbord, which combines to form bountiful wildlife habitat. Throughout the preserve you will hear a perpetual medley of bird songs: the rat-a-tat tapping of woodpeckers among the oaks, the strident caw of steller jays in the redwood groves, and the piercing call of red-tailed hawks circling high above the grasslands.

Signs of deer, bobcats, coyotes, and other mammals attest to this area's value to wildlife.

Springtime brings an exceptional number and variety of wild-flowers. Pink filaree flowers carpet the grassy slopes, mixed with blue-eyed grass, checkerbloom, buttercup, lupine, poppies, and wild cucumber. I was particularly impressed by the dense clusters of Douglas iris where grassland and oak woods meet.

As of this writing, parts of the main dirt road trail, near the power lines, are nearly impassable because of dense brush. Fortunately, this section can be easily avoided by taking cow trails across the grass-land and reconnecting with the trail to the east. Adventurous trail users may want to explore the many old ranch and logging roads in various stages of disrepair.

Following the route on the map you will encounter a wooden fence near a water tank. This area has several residences and is closed to the public. All buildings and immediate vicinities are closed to the public.

This preserve is open from dawn to dusk.

Slender Salamander

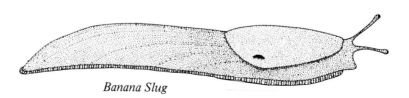

Banana Slug

Long Ridge Open Space

TO GET THERE . . . park at the Grizzly Flat turnout on Skyline Boulevard, 3 miles south of Page Mill Road, and 3.5 miles north of Saratoga Gap (Skyline and Highway 9). The turnout is identified by a gate and wooden fence, and is near a "Palo Alto City Limit" sign.

Long Ridge is one of the most beautiful and walkable places in the Santa Cruz Mountains. It has spectacular ridgetop views, grassy hills, shady wooded canyons, and a delightful pond that makes a perfect place for lunch. Most of the trails are former ranch roads.

The southern part of this 977-acre preserve includes Hickory Oak

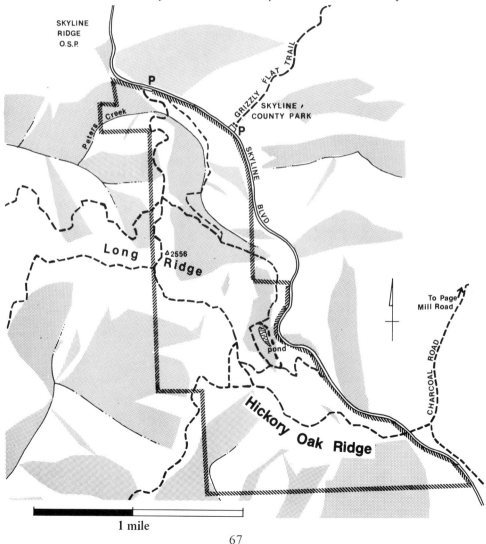

Ridge, which is accessible from Skyline Boulevard at a metal gate 1.6 miles north of Highway 9. Parking is limited. Stately groves of oak, madrone, and Douglas fir crown this beautiful ridge, with sweeping views of the mountains and ocean an added attraction. On a very clear day I was able to see as far as the Farallon Islands. I have also found this to be a great place to look for signs of wildlife. A dirt road trail follows the ridge crest.

A beautiful pond lies on the boundary between the preserve and land owned by a Zen Buddhist retreat. The Buddhists are friendly and allow walkers to loop around the pond and back up the ridge. The trail going downstream from the pond would form part of an ideal loop walk around the preserve if not for a wedge of private land blocking the route. As of this writing the owners lack the Buddhists' tolerance for foot travelers.

This preserve has been expanded westward to the boundary of Portola State Park, though they have not yet been connected by trail.

Dog owners will be glad to know that their pets are allowed on leash at the grassy area at the Grizzly Flat entrance.

For more information contact the Midpeninsula Regional Open Space District at (415) 949-5500.

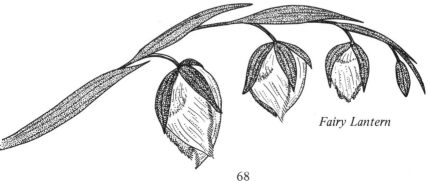

Fairy Lantern

68

Los Trancos Open Space

TO GET THERE... take **Page Mill Road 5 miles west from Highway 280. The parking lot is uphill from Foothill Park and about 1 mile east of Skyline Boulevard.**

This 274 acre park, with about 5 miles of trails, is one of my favorite nature study areas. An easy trail loops through grasslands, chaparral, and oak woods, and offers sweeping views of the bay, Mount Diablo, and San Francisco. Los Trancos straddles a revealing part of the 600 mile long San Andreas Fault, and displays many features that evidence fault activity. The trail passes Los Trancos Creek, which follows an old line of broken rock within the San Andreas fault zone. Posts with yellow bands and tops mark the location of known fault fractures.

Sag ponds, pressure ridges, and terraces in the park were created by the buckling of the rock under pressure from fault movement. Near the parking lot you will find conglomerate rocks that were sheared from Loma Prieta, a mountain 25 miles to the south, and were transported here by the gradual movement of land along the fault. The

(Continued on page 71)

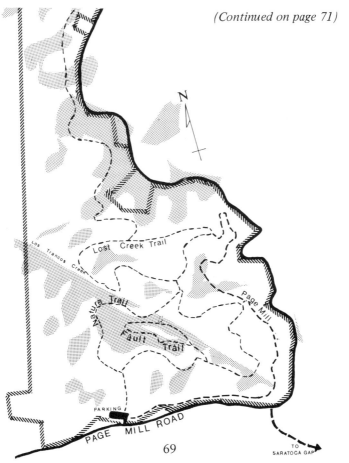

The Last Grizzly

Grizzly bears were once common in the Santa Cruz Mountains, feasting on berries and acorns, digging for roots, and gathering along streams to fish during the annual runs of salmon and steelhead. Their diet was nearly identical to that of the Ohlone Indians, who feared and revered the great bears.

But this was an abundant land, with a mild climate, and there was food enough for all. In fact, California probably had more grizzlies than anywhere else.

When the Spanish grazed cattle over their vast ranchos in the late eighteenth and early nineteenth centuries the opportunistic bears acquired a taste for beef.

This was a banquet that ended abruptly though, soon after California became a state in 1850. Gold, climate, and land brought hordes of immigrants to the Bay Area, including loggers and ranchers who claimed the Santa Cruz Mountains for their commercial value, leaving dwindling habitat for both grizzlies and Ohlone. The bears were shot on sight through the 1860's, 70's, and into the 1880's, when the last one was killed.

Around Bonny Doon Mountain lived an old sow bear who had acquired a taste for pork. Late one night in November of 1885 she made the mistake of carrying off a 300-pound hog that rancher Orrin Blodgett had been fattening for market. When Orrin found the remains that the bear had stashed away for later consumption he readied his rifle and waited. Several nights passed before the bear returned; and when she did, the rancher met up with her unexpectedly, with barely enough time to raise his muzzle-loaded rifle and fire—or at least that's his side of the story.

The dead bear weighed in at 642 pounds; the last grizzly ever reported in the Santa Cruz Mountains.

(Continued from page 69)

earth's crust is divided into massive plates of rock floating in the earth's mantle—and this is where 2 of them scrape together. East of here is the North American continental plate, and west is the Pacific plate. Naturalist tours leave from the parking lot on Sundays, and they are well worth attending. For more information, call the Midpeninsula Regional Open Space District at (415) 949-5500.

This is one of the Bay Area's most brilliant wildflower gardens in April when iridescent fields of blue-eyed grass, poppies, buttercups, and many others form a flowery carpet. This is also a good kite flying and picnicking spot. Madrone and bay trees are common here, as are black, blue, canyon live, and coast live oaks.

Los Trancos can be used as a starting point for exploring other open space preserves to the south, and you can even hike about 8 miles from here to Saratoga Gap, where the "Skyline-to-the-Sea" trail begins. This trans-park route can be started on Page Mill Road just downhill from the parking lot.

McNee Ranch State Park

TO GET THERE. . . take Highway 1 just north of Montara and park at the Martini Creek parking lot (8.1 miles north of Highway 92). It is across from a group of cypress trees. Walk carefully along the highway for a fifth of a mile to a white metal gate, where a dirt road enters the park.

This is one of the least known parks in the Santa Cruz Mountains, and it is in danger of being sliced in two by a proposed re-routing of Highway 1. As of this writing its fate is still in the courts.

McNee Ranch sweeps down the steep slopes of Montara Mountain to just above the vertical cliffs of Devil's Slide. Views of the ocean and mountains are seen from the ranch roads that make up the trail system. The hills are covered mainly with coastal scrub.

Be aware that strong and cold Pacific winds and dense fog lash these exposed slopes. So be prepared for changing conditions even on calm sunny days.

McNee Ranch shares an eastern boundary with San Pedro Valley County Park and the San Francisco Fish and Game Refuge.

The expedition of Spanish explorer Gaspar de Portola camped on the bank of Martini Creek on October 30, 1769, just prior to their discovery of San Francisco Bay.

Open from dawn to dusk, this park has none of the facilities you might expect at a state park. For more information, call the San Mateo Coast District of the California Department of Parks and Recreation at (415) 726-6203.

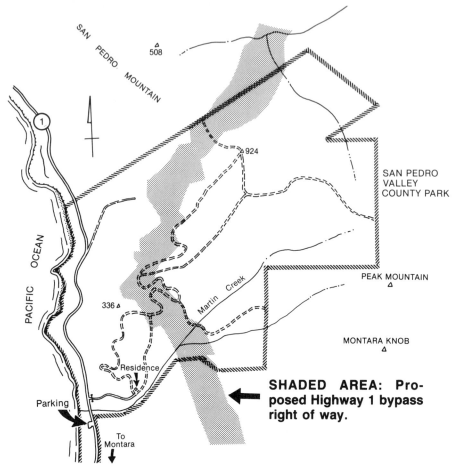

SAN PEDRO MOUNTAIN

Δ 508

1

PACIFIC OCEAN

SAN PEDRO VALLEY COUNTY PARK

Δ 924

Martin Creek

336 Δ

PEAK MOUNTAIN
Δ

MONTARA KNOB
Δ

Residence

SHADED AREA: Proposed Highway 1 bypass right of way.

Parking

To Montara

The Montara Hostel, 1.4 miles south of the park entrance, is a good and inexpensive place to spend the night. For information, call them at (415) 728-7177,

Some hillsides in this park have been severely eroded by illegal off-road motorcycle use.

Monte Bello Open Space

TO GET THERE . . . take Page Mill Road about 5 miles west from Highway 280 to the parking area just downhill from the Los Trancos parking lot.

The largest unit of the Midpeninsula Regional Open Space District, Monte Bello is a large and varied land of deep wooded canyons, windswept grassy ridges, and the San Andreas Fault.

With 13 miles of well-maintained trails, this 3,258-acre preserve is the hub of a lot of walking opportunities. Los Trancos Open Space is just across Page Mill Road; the Duveneck Windmill Pasture Area is reached by trail via the Black Mountain Trail; Saratoga Gap Open Space is just to the south, with trail connections to Skyline Ridge, Long Ridge, Russian Ridge and Coal Creek open space preserves. It's about 8 miles from Page Mill Road to Saratoga Gap (Skyline Boulevard/Highway 9 intersection); and from there another 28 miles to the ocean.

From the parking area on Page Mill (near Los Trancos parking) take the 3-mile Stevens Creek Nature Trail, which descends into a wooded canyon and then climbs past gnarled old oaks and through an abandoned walnut orchard. Pick up a brochure for the self-guided walk at the parking area. Next to the Canyon Trail, which goes all the way to Saratoga Gap, is a marshy sag pond filled with cattails and other aquatic plants. This pond is right on a fracture of the San Andreas Fault, and was formed when the land dropped. Evidence of fault movement is common nearby, where the unstable ground is landsliding.

The section of this trail from the parking lot to the Vista Point Overlook is being made wheelchair accessible.

If you wander off the beaten paths you may come across a deteriorating old tepee, a children's swing set, and a lot of other relics from the late 1960s and early 1970s when this was a commune called "The Land."

The Indian Creek Fire Trail is one of the preserve's more vigorous walks, climbing the Monte Bello Ridge for commanding vistas of the Bay Area and the Santa Cruz Mountains. From here you can explore the Monte Bello Fire Trail, or take the Black Mountain Trail down to the Duveneck Windmill Pasture Area and Hidden Villa.

Just west of Black Mountain is the Black Mountain Ranch Trailcamp. What a place to sleep: coyote serenades, with owl counterpoint melodies; and the whole urban spectacle sprawled out below. Camping here is by permit only and open fires are prohibited. Camp stoves are allowed. For permits and information, call the open space office.

As better parking facilities are provided on Page Mill Road, there will be more docent walks to help the public unravel the geological and ecological mysteries of this preserve. And I also hope there will eventually be better public access to the other end of the preserve at the uphill end of Monte Bello Road, via Stevens Canyon Road, from Cupertino. This area has excellent trails and some of the most striking views in the Santa Cruz Mountains. Docent tours for 5 to 25 people can be scheduled by calling the open space district office. This 3.5-mile guided walk is jammed with scenery and history, and you may be able to stop at one of several wineries just down the road on your way back.

The habitat diversity of this land makes it perfect for lots of wildlife, including bobcats, coyotes, deer, raccoons, and a wide variety of birds. Even mountain lions are known to patrol this region.

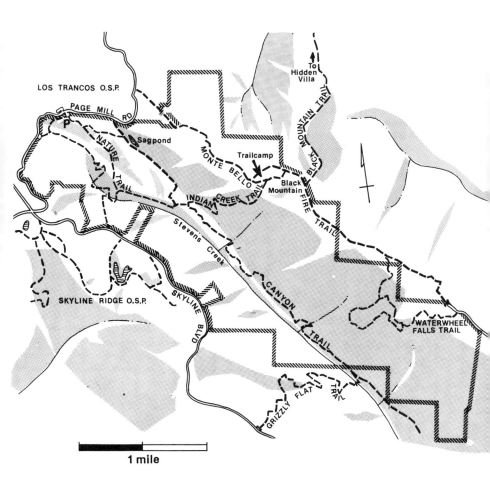

Call the Midpeninsula Regional Open Space District at (415) 949-5500 for information on guided walks through this park.

Picnicking on the San Andreas Fault.

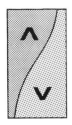 

The sag pond is one of many features of the San Andreas Fault, where the North American Plate meets the Pacific Plate. Where the fault is curved, fault movement creates sagging gaps where ponds sometimes form.

Mount Madonna County Park

TO GET THERE. . .take Hecker Pass Highway (Route 152) west from Gilroy.

This is a park for people who like scenic diversity, panoramic vistas, and steep trails. The park has more than 17 miles of foot and bridle trails which explore peaceful groves of redwood and oak, snake through scratchy expanses of chaparral, and gallop across open grassy hills. The park has 3,093 acres and plenty of room for even the most undauntable of hikers. To further tax your energy, it straddles a ridge-top and few of the trails come anywhere close to being level.

One of the steepest trails goes to Sprig Lake, a small but deep reservoir open to fishing by visitors between the ages of 5 and 12.

The Merry-Go-Round Trail is a steep and scenic whirlwind tour of all the park's ecological communities. It is especially pleasant in early spring when the grassy areas at the lower elevations turn green and are splashed with flowery colors. A 5 mile loop can be made by combining the Miller, Loop, Merry-Go-Round, Contour, and Ridge trails. Begin the hike just past park headquarters at the end of the road.

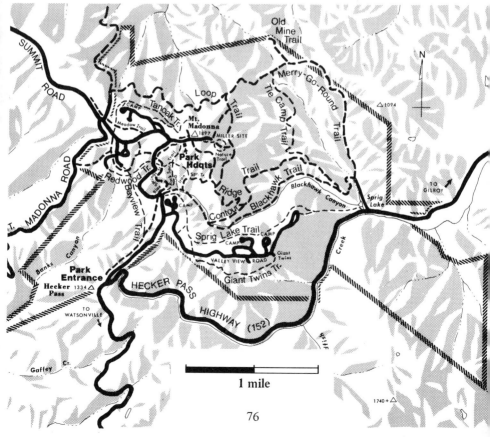

1 mile

Redwoods thrive in the coastal fog, which reduces evaporation through the critical drought months by lowering air temperatures and by lessening the exposure to direct sunlight. It makes another important contribution that most people would never guess: "fog drip". Heavy fog condenses into little water droplets on the needles of redwood trees and then drip down to other drops below, picking up momentum and dropping to the ground like a regular rainfall. This can be an important source of moisture, especially in summer, and an unfortunate hazard for unwary campers. Several summers ago I car camped under a redwood tree in this park, having failed to bring a tent because of our lack of summer rain. About 3 a.m. I awoke wet and cold and hastily ran to my car to escape what I though was a rare and rather heavy summer rain. The next morning, to my surprise, I saw that only the area immediately under the redwood tree was wet, and that I would have kept dry if I had slept just 30 feet away.

Picnicking and camping facilities are available on a first-come, first-served basis. For information, call park headquarters at (408) 842-2341.

Pescadero Creek County Park

TO GET THERE. . .it is accessible from San Mateo Memorial and Sam McDonald county parks and Portola State Park.

This is a large forested park on the watershed of one of the Santa Cruz Mountains' major creeks. For years this 6,000-acre park was used largely for reaching adjoining parks; but now there are two trail camps which make Pescadero a major target for backpackers. From Sam McDonald County Park, Tarwater Flat Trailcamp is 5 miles, and Shaw Flat Trailcamp is 4 miles. For reservations, call (415) 363-4021.

A trail connecting San Mateo County Memorial Park and Portola State Park passes through Pescadero Creek County Park. Finding the trail may be a problem, so be sure to ask directions at park headquarters if in doubt. The approximately 6 mile trail from Memorial Park can be started at the swimming area by the dam on Pescadero Creek. Follow Pescadero Creek Trail east to Wurr Road at the bridge and turn right, continuing the route south a short distance to a small wooden bridge on the left side of the road. The fire road which begins here continues through Pescadero Creek County Park.

The entrance to Portola State Park is the first fire road to the left beyond the fire road to the Sherriff's Honor Camp. The route is well maintained and easy to follow once it has been found, and can even be bicycled. The grade is relatively level, requiring little strenuous hiking, and a moderately fit hiker should be able to hike one way in about 3 hours.

Pescadero Creek County Park was heavily logged earlier in this century and today has few virgin redwoods, and evidence of logging is still visible. Rusting logging cables can still be found wrapped around redwood trunks and notches for loggers' springboards can still be found on old redwood stumps. It has been estimated that the Santa Cruz Mountains have yielded more than 10 billion feet of lumber since the Gold Rush. This land was acquired by the county to be dammed and flooded by a reservoir. When the plan was abandoned the land became a park.

A permit to enter this park may be obtained at either San Mateo County Memorial Park or at Sam McDonald County Park.

SEE MAP ON PAGE 82

Pescadero Marsh Preserve

TO GET THERE . . . take Highway 1 to Pescadero Road, just west of the town of Pescadero. There are parking accesses on Highway 1 at Pescadero State Beach and on Pescadero Road.

Pescadero Creek and Butano Creek flow together to form the largest coastal marsh between Monterey Bay and the Golden Gate. The short trails that run along the 640 acres of wetlands, provide bountiful opportunities for seeing such birds as least and spotted sandpipers, godwits, great egrets, herons, and migrating waterfowl. Several short trails offer birding opportunities among the preserve's cattails, tules, and willows.

Upstream erosion from logging and agriculture are causing serious sedimentation that will hasten the end of the marsh if action is not taken. Though part of the state park system, California has done little to protect or restore this preserve.

Picchetti Ranch Open Space

TO GET THERE . . . from Highway 280 take South Foothill Blvd. and Stevens Canyon Road south and turn west on Monte Bello Road.

This 307-acre preserve offers a leisurely walk through the late nineteenth century and an easy blend of natural and agrarian qualities.

There are only about 2 miles of trails here, and all are broad and of easy grade. You can walk through orchards of apricots, plums, walnuts, and pears to the small pond, where waterfowl gather in winter. In spring the fruit trees and wildflowers blossom and apricots may be eaten in early summer. Look for wild roses along this trail.

Heading north from the pond area the trails make a gentle ascent to an oakwooded hilltop overlook of Stevens Creek Reservoir and the Santa Clara Valley.

This preserve is named for the Italian immigrants Vincenzo and Secondo Picchetti, who built the original homestead house in 1882. The large yellow ranch house was built in 1886, and the brick winery was added in 1896. It operated under the Picchetti Brothers label until 1963. After 20 years of disrepair, these buildings, which are listed in in the National Register of Historic Places, have been restored by Sunrise Winery, which leases the buildings.

The winery area is open on Saturdays for wine tasting and tours on other days by special arrangements. The rest of the preserve is open daily from dawn to dusk.

Though a separate piece of property, this preserve is administered as part of Monte Bello Open Space. For more information call the Mid-peninsula Regional Open Space District at (415) 949-5500.

Sunrise Winery is open to the public Friday, Saturday, and Sunday from 11 a.m. to 3 p.m.

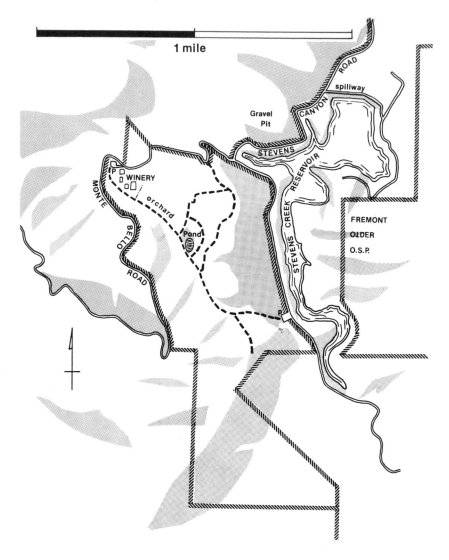

"I find that the three truly great times for thinking thoughts are when I am standing in the shower, sitting on the john, or walking. And the greatest of these, by far, is walking."

— Colin Fletcher

Portola State Park

**TO GET THERE. . .take Alpine Road west from Skyline Boulevard
and turn south on Portola State Park Road.**

Since 1945 Bay Area hikers have been exploring this redwood-
forested park along Pescadero Creek. Its 2,100 acres offer more than
10 miles of trails through mostly second-growth redwood groves,
though a few stands of big trees somehow survived. The park also offers
opportunities for car and trail camping, fishing, and swimming.

The park's self-guided nature loop trail, which can be started just
behind park headquarters, is a good place to start hiking. Though it's
less than a mile long, the Sequoia Trail can be connected with the Iverson Trail for a more extensive hike. The main reason for making a point
of exploring this little loop trail is to see the Shell Tree, one of the
Santa Cruz Mountains' most amazing sights. The tree has an impressive
17 foot diameter—yet what is most striking about it is that it seems to
be a structural impossibility. The ancient tree, estimated to be at least
2,000 years old, has been completely gutted by fire, and with only a
few narrow strands of living tissue reaching the ground it is a marvel
that green leaves still grow from its lofty branches.

From here you can hike the Iverson Trail along Pescadero Creek,
which contains water all year and has a wading pool near the visitors
center. A 6 mile public trail (actually a fire road) connects Portola
State Park with San Mateo County Memorial Park. The trail goes
through Pescadero Creek County Park and can be reached from the
Iverson Trail where it intersects a fire road southeast of Iverson Creek.
This route begins beside Iverson Cabin, built in 1860, and continues
uphill to its intersection with the fire road to San Mateo Memorial
and Sam McDonald parks.

The Summit and Slate Creek trails can be combined to form an
enjoyable hike of about 8.5 miles. The Summit Trail can be reached
from the Redwood Trail which begins across the road from the Point
Group Camp Area. This route goes to Slate Creek, Page Mill Site, and
to a fine stand of redwoods near the trail's end at the park boundary.
Before reaching the Page Mill Site there is a trailcamp about 3 miles
from the trailhead at the intersection of Slate Creek Trail and a fire
road.

One of the most impressive old-growth redwood groves left in
the Santa Cruz Mountains was recently added to this park. Unfortunately, though, this 350-acre parcel on Peters Creek has no trail access,
and the dense underbrush makes cross-country hiking difficult. A trail
is planned. Another trail being planned will connect Portola with Big
Basin.

For information and reservations, call park headquarters at (415)
948-9098.

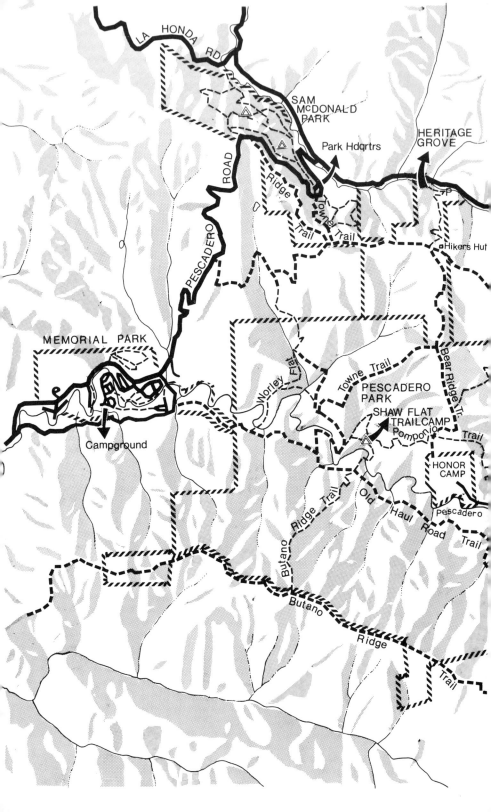

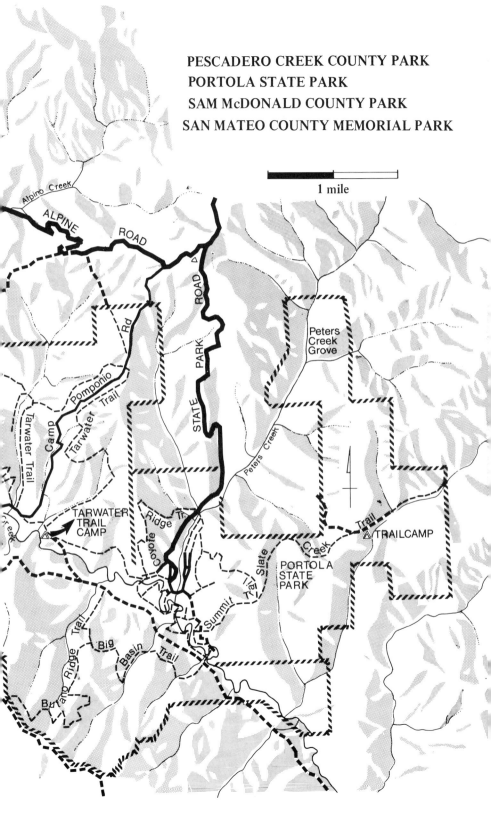

PESCADERO CREEK COUNTY PARK
PORTOLA STATE PARK
SAM McDONALD COUNTY PARK
SAN MATEO COUNTY MEMORIAL PARK

1 mile

Purisima Creek Open Space

TO GET THERE. . . on Skyline Boulevard, 4.5 miles south of Highway 92, the parking area is about 200 feet south of the Alpen Rose Restaurant. The east end of Purisima Creek Road is about half a mile north of Kings Mountain Road. From Highway 1, just south of Half Moon Bay, take Higgins-Purisima Road 4.5 miles to an entrance gate by a small bridge.

Climbing 1600 feet of steep terrain just east of Skyline Boulevard, this preserve has the northernmost major redwood forest in the Santa Cruz Mountains. In fact, it is the only one of the open space district lands with substantial redwood groves.

This 2,509-acre preserve also is wooded with Douglas fir, madrone, chaparral, and has lots of ridgetop views of the Pacific and the local mountains. Be prepared for a workout on about 10 miles of mostly steep trails.

Purisima Canyon is a major east-west drainage, with a perennial creek. Though the area was logged intensively between the 1850's and 1920, supporting 7 sawmills for awhile, the second-growth forest now rises tall, and stumps up to 16 feet in diameter remind us of the great trees that were cut.

There are still some majestic stands of large, first-growth redwoods in the park, however, though you won't find them along the park's main trails, which were built as logging roads. In a few areas too inaccessible for loggers, hardy hikers can still find some magnificent old giants. One such place is up Whittemore Gulch where the old road-bed along the creek peters out into a narrow trail and finally into scarcely any kind of a trail at all (at least as of this writing). Here stands a grove of great trees as remote and primeval as any to be found in the Santa Cruz Mountains. Another grove of virgin redwoods stands

For a spectacular, though physically-demanding 6-mile loop around Whittemore Gulch, combine the Jeep Trail, the new foot trail into Whittemore Gulch, and the Harkins Fire Trail. This route involves an elevation range of about 1,400 feet.

A special trail for the physically handicapped has been built just off Skyline Boulevard north of Kings Mountain Road near where Purisima Creek Road intersects Skyline.

Open space docent Ernie Ramires at one of the remaining big trees up Whittemore Gulch.

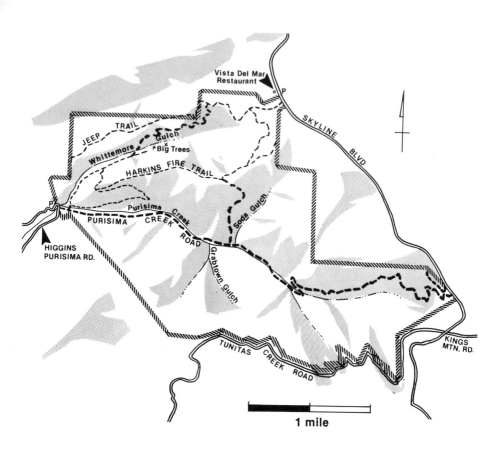

1 mile

The distance between Skyline Boulevard and Higgins-Purisima Road via the Purisima Creek Road Trail requires a walk of about 3 miles and an altitude change of about 1600 feet. Unfortunately, this route will require backtracking, unless you arrange car shuttles between the upper and lower parts of the park. This beautiful and forested canyon was acquired with the help of the Save The Redwoods League.

This park provides an essential link in the proposed "City-to-the-Sea" trail, which begins at Edgewood County Park in Redwood City, follows the Crystal Springs Trail to Huddart Park, climbs to Skyline, and then down through Purisima Canyon to Higgins-Purisima Road. All of the trails needed for this crossing of the Santa Cruz Mountains already exist. It is ideal for equestrians as well as walkers.

Being on the coast side of Skyline, be prepared for windy and foggy weather. For more information, call the Midpeninsula Regional Open Space District at (415) 949-5500.

Rancho San Antonio Open Space

TO GET THERE . . . from **Highway 280 take Foothill Boulevard south and turn west on Cristo Rey Drive. Parking is in the adjacent Rancho San Antonio County Park**.

With easy access to the Mountain View, Los Altos, and Cupertino vicinity, this is the most popular of the open space preserves. It's a perfect destination for walking, running, and picnicking. A well-established system of gentle trails will take you throughout the nearly 1000 acres of this preserve.

Historic Deer Hollow Farm is one of the park's most popular features and is used for a variety of environmental education programs by the city of Mountain View, which leases the farm. For more information, call (415) 966-6331. It is especially popular with children. These old nineteenth-century farm buildings were built by the Grant brothers, who purchased the land in 1860 for cattle ranching.

This is one of the few parks in the low foothills on the east side of the range. With an elevation ranging from 400 to over 1,400 feet, this area is characterized by chaparral and grasslands and by oak woodlands composed of several species of oak, bay, madrone, and buckeye. Wildflowers cover the grassy hillsides in early spring. The oaks here are excellent for climbing, and a rest stop in the shade of their sprawling limbs may help you appreciate why the Druids of ancient Gaul and Britain considered oak forests to be the most sacred of places.

The park is managed to provide a balance between recreational and agricultural use. A working farm remains on the property and cattle

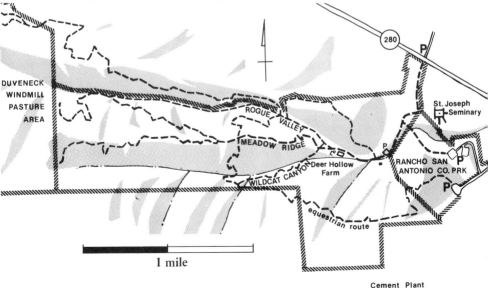

The animals at Deer Hollow Farm help to make Rancho San Antonio one of the most popular open space preserves.

graze on the grasslands. But they don't seem to bother the yellow meadowlark or deter the black-tail deer, which are common here. You may also see piles of sticks, resembling beaver hutches, which are the home of dusky-footed woodrats. Most of the Park's trails are old ranch roads which may be explored by foot, horse, or bicycle.

Sycamores, willows, alders, box elders, and dogwoods are among the streamside trees whose foliage merges together, often covering creeks and making them invisible even from above. Hikers should take note that thorny blackberry vines, fallen tree limbs, and dense tree and shrub growth often make riperian woodlands tough to explore without trails.

The 375-acre western part of the preserve, which connects the original preserve with the Duveneck Windmill Pasture Area, was added in 1984. This area, covering a long and grassy ridge with views of the Santa Clara Valley, may be explored by taking the Meadow Ridge Trail.

Russian Ridge Open Space

TO GET THERE . . . from **Highway 280** take **Page Mill Road** uphill and west to where it intersects **Skyline Boulevard**. **The preserve begins at the northwest corner of the intersection. Another access is at the vista point turnoff on Skyline a little over a mile to the north.**

This combination of canyon woodland and high, grassy promontories is the perfect place for casual saunters. Don't let the absence of a formal trail system deter you. This 1,354-acre preserve is a place to explore; replete with unconnected cow and deer trails and the faint traces of ranch roads that make ideal footpaths.

If you don't like what passes here for trails, blaze your own. Head out footloose over the grassy slopes, exploring the bay, oak, and buckeye groves that are neatly creased into the folds of the ridge; but try not to stray onto private lands bordering the preserve. Remember, if you have to climb through or over a barbed wire fence, you are probably trespassing.

For a more structured ramble, walk the old ranch road on the spine of the ridge. It can be reached by ascending the hill at the southern access or by entering the dirt road gate entrance at the vista point and heading uphill. This route offers an overview of the whole preserve, visiting the highest points and unfolding a 360-degree panoramic display of Mount Tamalpais and San Francisco to the north; the bay and Mount Diablo to the east; Mount Umunhum and Monterey Bay to the south; and the ocean to the west.

This is an outstanding place to see wildflowers in the Spring. After a winter rain I found enormous spherical mushrooms more than a foot in diameter on a boulder-crowned promontory, looking very much like boulders themselves. This is also an ideal place for skiing on those rare winter days when snow mantles the hills. With its smooth, rounded forms, Russian Ridge offers miles of cross-country skiing – and some surprisingly good downhill runs too. Keep your skis ready at a moment's notice between December and February. Conditions may only be good for a few hours, usually in the early morning.

Ohlone Indians prepared acorns on these ancient grinding stones at Russian Ridge.

Parking

COAL CREEK
OPEN SPACE

LANGLEY HILL
QUARRY RD.

Mt.
Melville
2195

Coal Creek

Coal Creek

CRAZY PETE'S ROAD

ALPINE ROAD

Corte Madera Creek

LOS
TRANCOS
OPEN
SPACE

SKYLINE

Parking

Waterfall

Private

PAGE MILL ROAD

Vista Point
Parking

BLVD.

MONTE BELLO
OPEN SPACE

RUSSIAN RIDGE
OPEN SPACE

Borel Hill
2572

Private

Mindego Creek

ALPINE ROAD

Parking

Alpine
Pond

SKYLINE RIDGE OPEN SPACE

1 mile

This park has exceptionally large and beautiful manzanita.

Saint Joseph's Hill Park

TO GET THERE. . . from Highway 17 take Alma Bridge Road at Lexington Reservoir, cross the dam and park at the first parking lot on the right. To enter the park walk uphill on the dirt road across from the parking lot.

There aren't enough miles of trails in this park to keep you going for long, unless you slow down and make frequent stops to enjoy the scenery. The ranch road trail to the 1,253-foot summit of Saint Joseph's

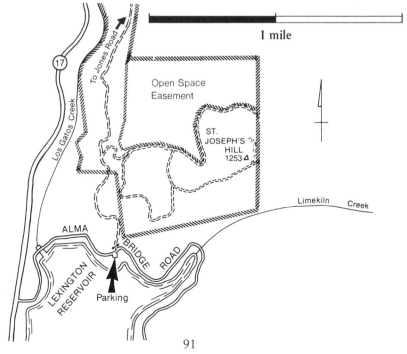

Hill is just steep enough to get the blood pulsing, but not far enough for a serious workout.

On the way up you will find increasingly attractive views of Lexington Reservoir and the surrounding mountains. The trail passes through splendid groves of exceptionally large manzanita bushes. They seem to prefer to grow in the areas of serpentine, a rock easily identified by its smooth and waxy feel.

Part of the trail is bordered by a chain link fence which keeps visitors from wandering onto property owned by The California Province of the Society of Jesus. The entire park is only 170 acres, though it seems much bigger because of the grandiose views. An additional 97 acres are retained by the Jesuits to be left undeveloped under an open space easement.

Near the summit the chaparral suddenly yields to a grassland area that the Jesuits once used as a vineyard. The top of Saint Joseph's Hill is a wonderful place for a picnic and a nap. A 360-degree panorama offers views of Mount Hamilton, the Diablo Range, and the Santa Clara Valley to the east; San Francisco Bay and the cities of the Peninsula to the north; and the ridges and peaks of the Santa Cruz Mountains and Lexington Reservoir to the west and south.

For more information contact the Midpeninsula Regional Open Space District at (415) 949-5500.

Off-Road Bicycling

Non-motorized, off-road bicycle use has been nearly doubling each year, making this the fastest growing group of trail users.

These vehicles are generating a lot of controversy and increasing restrictions in the Santa Cruz Mountains. Public agencies responsible for public lands are receiving complaints from walkers, equestrians, and joggers about cyclists going too fast around blind turns and on narrow trails. Several injuries have occurred.

There is also concern about trail erosion caused by narrow linear soil compaction that channels water flow. This is particularly a problem on steep trails during the rainy season.

The solution to this problem may be to limit bicycles to dirt road trails that already have compacted soils and to encourage cyclists to take responsibility for maintaining certain trails for their use. Because most public agencies are still formulating policies on off-road bicycle use, the minority of riders causing safety and other problems threaten to further limit trail use for all cyclists.

Policies concerning off-road bicycle use:

Midpeninsula Regional Open Space Preserves: *All trails are open to bicycle use except for those marked otherwise at trailheads.*

State Parks: *At this time bicycles are not allowed on park trails, though specially designed trails for cyclists are being considered.*

Santa Clara County Parks: *As of this writing Santa Clara County still has no policy on off-road bicycles. Scientific studies of environmental and sociological impact are being conducted which will help to identify trails that can safely accommodate these vehicles. For current information call (408) 358-3741.*

San Mateo County Parks: *Off-road bicycles are permitted only on the following trails:*

- *Pescadero Creek County Park—Pomponio Road, Bridge Trail, Old Haul Road.*
- *San Bruno Mountain County Park—Saddle Loop Trail, Day Camp Access Trail.*
- *Sawyer Camp Trail.*
- *San Pedro Valley County Park—Weiler Ranch Road.*

Golden Gate National Recreation Area: *Bicycles are allowed on fire roads on Sweeney Ridge.*

Sam McDonald County Park

TO GET THERE. . .take La Honda-Pescadero Road about 3 miles west of La Honda.

This is a beautiful 860 acres of redwoods and an ideal destination for a picnic and a hike. The park is kept in a semi-primitive state by limiting automobile access only to the park office area off Pescadero Road. Three walk-in campgrounds, available by reservation, range in distance from .5 to about 1 mile from the parking lot.

The McDonald Trail loop is a good 3.1 mile hike northwest from the parking lot, and though not very long, this peaceful redwood garden of sorrel and ferns has plenty of scenic diversions and its share of challenging ups and downs. The continuation of the McDonald Trail beginning on the other side of the parking lot is equally rewarding. This part of the trail continues as a dirt road for about 2 miles southwest from Pescadero Road and passes some splendid first-growth redwoods, the most magnificent of which can be seen along the short footpath that crosses and then returns back to the dirt road. The route climbs the steep hillside to the top of the ridge, where redwoods give way to grassy areas and oak trees.

Campers who prefer an artificial sky to the real one may want to stay in the Sierra Club's hikers hut on the ridge about a mile from the parking lot. This small structure, which was shipped from Denmark in prefabricated pieces, has an electric stove, water, a sleeping area, and an aerobic decay toilet. This is the first of what some people hope will be a series of shelters along the expanding trail system between the bay and the ocean. For more information and reservations, call the Sierra Club at (415) 327-8111.

Sam McDonald's southern boundary touches Pescadero Creek County Park which is reached by fire trail. From there it is possible to hike to Portola State Park and San Mateo Memorial Park.

This is one of the greenest and most densely forested of the redwood parks, but it is almost deserted during the winter months. The area was logged early in this century, but some of the grand old big trees survived.

Backpackers should consider hiking fire trails from Sam McDonald to Pescadero Creek and San Mateo Memorial county parks and Portola State Park. The hike is about 4.5 miles from Sam McDonald Park headquarters to the trail along Pescadero Creek which connects San Mateo Memorial and Portola Parks. The total distance to San Mateo Memorial County Park is about 6 miles, and to Portola State Park is a little more than 7 miles. This is a beautifully scenic trail that climbs past first and second-growth redwoods to grassy hilltop vistas and then descends into a forest of Douglas fir and second-growth redwoods. When you get to the top of the ridge, in the grassy meadow, head east on the intersecting ridge trail and continue until the road forks in 3 directions. Take the middle road and stay to the right until it crosses Pescadero Creek and intersects the fire road paralleling the creek. An alternative route back to the parking lot can be taken from here by heading west and north on the ridgetop dirt road, crossing Pescadero Road and hiking southeast by footpath.

The Sierra Club's hikers hut is a great place to stay.

The Towne Trail takes you from park headquarters to the hikers hut.

Sam McDonald (1884-1957) was a popular Stanford University employee who owned the property until his death. He loved nature and willed that his forest be preserved in its natural state. Stanford owned the land until it became a county park in 1969.

For more information and reservations for group camping, call park headquarters at (415) 747-0403.

Heritage Grove

This 37-acre, old-growth redwood grove adjoins Sam McDonald Park and can be reached by trail from the hikers' hut or by traveling east on Alpine Road one mile from its intersection with Pescadero Road. This magnificent grove was scheduled to be logged until a citizens group raised funds and purchased the land. The loggers' paint marks can still be seen on some of the trees they intended to remove. Several short nature trails make this a wonderful stroll through the redwoods.

SEE MAP ON PAGE 82

Walk for Health

Our bodies are perfectly designed for walking. There is no other form of exercise that is safer or more beneficial.

Vigorous walking maintains the heart muscle in healthy tone, lowers blood pressure, controls weight, reduces tension, headaches, and backaches; and it even benefits the heart and lungs every bit as much as jogging.

A Veterans Administration study of elderly people found that a walking program actually resulted in improved memory, vision, and reasoning power.

Doctors recommend taking a post-walk stroll for a few minutes after a vigorous outing to give the heart a chance to slow down gradually.

San Bruno Mountain County Park

TO GET THERE. . .take Bayshore Boulevard in Brisbane, turn west on Guadalupe Road, and south on Radio Road to the ridgetop.

This 1,314 foot high promontory is a grassland island in an urban sea and is the only large open space in this densely settled and industrialized area. It's an ecological remnant of northern San Mateo County and a wonderful wildflower garden in spring. Actually, this "mountain" consists of 2 parallel ridges separated by the Guadalupe Valley.

To explore the mountain, walk east on the Ridge Trail from the parking lot near the radio towers. This path offers at least 3 miles of walking round trip. Another trail system to the west, starting at Radio Road, forms a scenic and moderately easy 3-mile loop, with lots of views of the great urban expanses of San Francisco to the north, and South San Francisco and Daly City to the south.

This 2,000-acre park is home to at least 384 native plants and 2 rare butterflies. The Mission blue butterfly, already on the endangered species list, and the San Francisco silverspot, proposed for endangered species status, live here and have caused quite a controversy over housing development in the area. A compromise was reached when a major housing developer modified his design to ensure that there would be room for both people and butterflies.

Most of the mountain is covered with coastal scrub vegetation and with annual grasses that make it green in the winter and spring and golden brown in summer. Most of the trees are in the canyons and on north-facing slopes. A few coastal wood, bracken, and chain ferns dwell in moist and shady places.

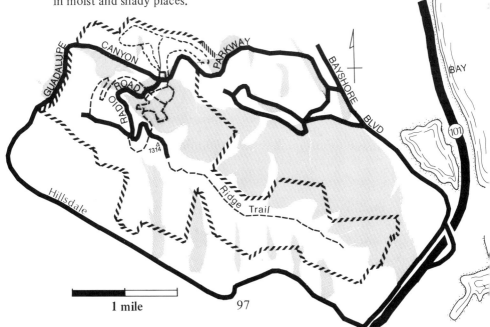

1 mile

The view from San Bruno Mountain.

San Francisco Fish and Game Refuge

If you've ever gazed into the land around Crystal Springs and San Andreas lakes while driving on Highway 280 and wished it were possible to get in there to explore, then you may be interested to know that there is some limited access. Because the city of San Francisco jealously guards the purity of its drinking water the walkways through this 23,000-acre watershed are wide and bordered with barbed wire fences, and some are paved.

Schools and educational groups, however, may obtain permits to visit other areas of the property for nature study. One such organization is Nature Explorations, (415) 324-8737, which frequently offers guided nature walks for the public. Applications for permits should be filed at least 2 weeks in advance by contacting the San Francisco Water Department at 1000 El Camino Real, Millbrae, CA 94030; (415) 679-4424, extension 212.

Sawyer Camp Road runs along Crystal Springs Reservoir.

CRYSTAL SPRINGS TRAIL:

The Crystal Springs hiking and riding trail connects Huddart Park with San Bruno Avenue in San Bruno. It goes from Huddart to Raymundo Road and resumes a fifth of a mile up the road, paralleling Highway 280 and Canada Road. The distance to San Bruno is 12 miles; to the Pulgas Water Temple is 4.2 miles. This route is popular with equestrians, though many walkers won't like the flatness and tameness of the route, or the sights and sounds of traffic on Highway 280 and Canada Road.

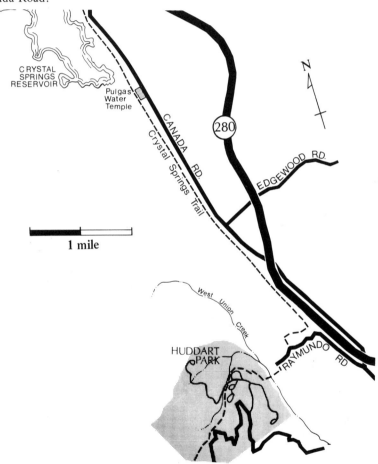

FILOLI ESTATE:

Surrounded by the San Francisco watershed property, the Filoli estate, with 16 acres of gardens, is owned by the National Trust for Historic Preservation. It was built for Mr. and Mrs. William B. Bourne II from 1916 to 1919. The entrance gate is south of the Pulgas Water Temple on Canada Road.

The house and garden are open for tours by appointment only, Tuesday through Saturday. There is an admission charge. For more information phone (415) 366-4640 or (415) 364-2171; or write: Friends of Filoli Tours, Canada Road, Woodside, CA 94062.

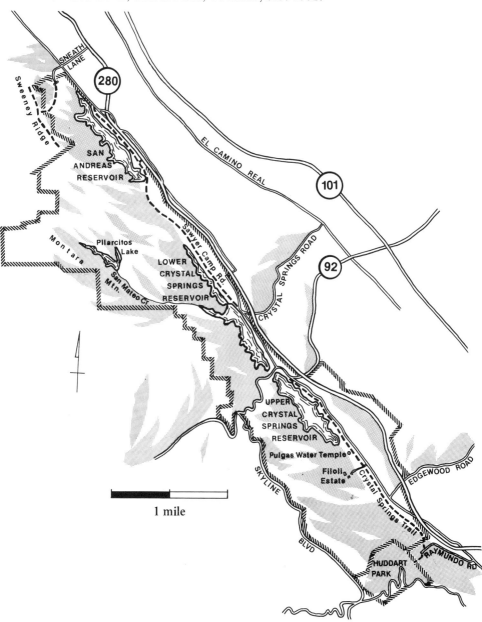

1 mile

SAWYER CAMP ROAD:

This scenic paved road is closed to motor vehicles. Access is from Skyline Boulevard at Hillcrest Boulevard, and at Crystal Springs Road. This 6-mile route is particularly popular with bicyclists.

SAN ANDREAS TRAIL:

This wide and relatively level trail runs 2.9 miles from the north end of the Sawyer Camp Road, at Hillcrest, to Skyline Boulevard. Most of the trail is paved.

SNEATH LANE:

From Highway 280 in San Bruno, take Sneath Lane west all the way to the locked gate. The paved road continues through the San Francisco watershed property, with barbed wire on both sides, and up the Sweeney Ridge unit of the Golden Gate National Recreation Area. This route offers great views of San Andreas Reservoir.

San Mateo County Memorial Park

TO GET THERE. . .it's southwest of Sam McDonald Park on Pescadero Road.

Visitors to San Mateo County Memorial Park may swim in Pescadero Creek, camp, picnic, and hike about 5 miles of trails. The park covers about 350 acres and has lots of beautiful redwoods and some interesting trails, though none of them are long enough to contain the enthusiasm of a good hiker. The Mount Ellen-Summit Trail-Lower Nature Trail loop around the summit of Mount Ellen is a scenic route involving a climb of about 400 feet and a hike of less than 2 miles.

If you're looking for something a bit more challenging than Memorial Park has to offer, try hiking to Portola State Park or Sam McDonald County Park, both about 6 miles away. For information on routes to these parks see the chapters on Pescadero Creek and Sam McDonald county parks.

This park has 140 family campsites, available on a first-come, first-served basis. For more information, call (415) 879-0212.

A TRAIL FOR THE DISABLED:

Memorial Park now has a trail designed for the physically disabled. Half a mile long, the Tanoak Nature Trail is level and smooth enough to be used by manual wheelchairs, and a cable runs along its edge to help blind people follow with a cane or dog. There are 14 stations along the trail, with guides available in large print, Braille, and tape cassettes explaining the beauty of the redwood forest.

Because of the popularity of this trail, there is interest in establishing additional trails for disabled people in the Santa Cruz Mountains. If you are interested in helping, contact the Whole Access Project, 1331 American Way, Menlo Park, CA 94025.

San Pedro Valley County Park

TO GET THERE. . .take **Highway 1 to Pacifica, heading southeast on Linda Mar Boulevard to Oddstad Boulevard. Public parking and park access are next to Saint Peters Catholic Church.**

This park is a 1,000 acre mass of coastal scrub and chaparral, with a few grassy places and riperian woodlands for diversity. You can get a look at it by hiking the dirt road along the Middle Fork of San Pedro Creek.

Keep an eye open for the footpath that switchbacks up the hillside from the dirt road, climbing to some nice views of the San Pedro Valley and winding around the hills for 1.6 miles and back to the dirt road. In the spring you will see scrub flowers, and the spicy aroma of sage lingers around the hills all year. Take some time to listen for the mingling melodies of birds.

The middle and south forks of San Pedro Creek flow year around and are among the few remaining spawning areas of steelhead trout in San Mateo County, especially from December to February. Views of Brooks Falls, which drops 175 feet in 3 tiers, may be enjoyed during the rainy season.

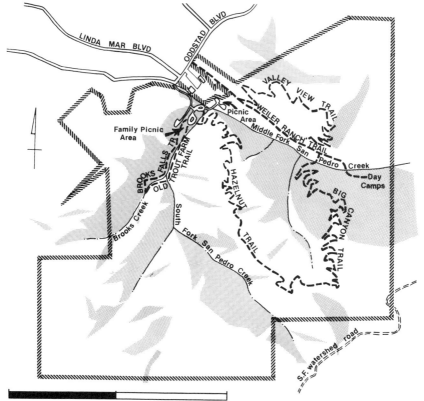

1 mile

This park has a combination of coastal scrub and true chaparral vegetation, and sometimes it is hard to tell them apart. The main difference is that they each have their own distinct assortment of plants. Both are composed of short, stiff, and thorny vegetation that is virtually impenetrable, which is why this park is not a good place for cross-country hiking. Unfortunately, San Pedro Valley County Park still has relatively few trails and needs a much more extensive trail system before it can be rated as a prime target for hikers.

The characteristic plant here is coyote brush, a modest shrub with deep roots and small, stiff leaves designed to conserve moisture. It is common along the coast where westerly ocean breezes blow unobstructed. Coyote brush produces small white flowers and has small waxy leaves.

Other common coastal scrub vegetation includes: monkeyflower, shrubby lupine, ceanothus, coastal sage scrub, and thimbleberry. This vegetation thrives in the coastal zone where steady ocean winds sweep the land and make life difficult for most trees. Along the park's small creeks you will notice dense stands of willows, which shelter a ground cover which includes poison hemlock, blackberry vines, horsetails, and bracken ferns.

This park has a group picnic area and family picnic sites with barbecue pits. Reservations are required for all youth groups, regardless of size or activity. The group picnic area is open by reservation, which may be obtained by calling (415) 363-4021.

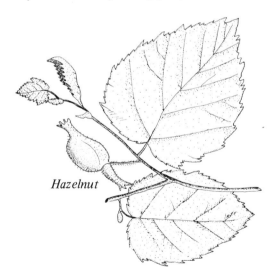

Hazelnut

TREE TOP CHALLENGES:

Have you ever considered climbing 50 feet up a redwood tree and then jumping? How about climbing up a 14-foot wall? These are just 2 of a variety of safe and even sane activities offered by Tree Tops Challenges near La Honda.

Starting the day with warm-up exercises, participants are introduced to progressively more challenging climbing and balancing events, from 6 inches to 60 feet off the ground. Right from the start each group is taught to act as a team, each participant helping and supporting each other.

This is a day you will never forget; and besides being a lot of fun the course teaches skills that are applicable back in the city, including leadership, confidence, communication, and the ability to work together as a group. I was amazed to discover that I could do things that I never would have thought possible.

The Ropes Course is conducted by Tree Top Challenges, 524 Collins Ave., Colma, CA 94014; (415) 756-7250.

Sanborn Skyline County Park

TO GET THERE... take **Highway 9 (Big Basin Way) west from Saratoga and turn south on Sanborn Road.**

Sanborn Skyline County Park covers 2,856 acres on the steep east side of the range and has scenic trails, excellent picnicking facilities, a walk-in campground, and one of the Bay Area's best hostels. From the park's many scenic overlooks you can gaze down on the smoggy haze that often covers San Jose and instead be glad to be in the mountains.

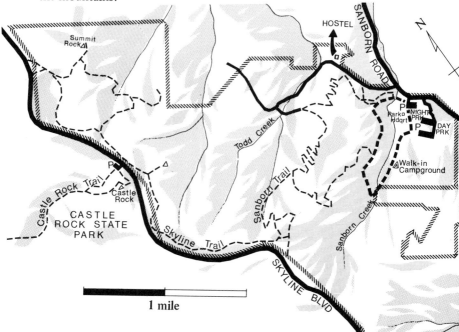

1 mile

The park has 2 entrances from Sanborn Road, one for day use and another for camping. There are 42 campsites on the Sanborn Trail, available on a first-come, first-served basis. To camp at these sites park at the overnight parking lot, register at the nearby park headquarters, and walk the short distance uphill from the parking lot to the camping area. Each family campsite has a picnic table, a fire place, and restrooms nearby.

Park headquarters are in an interesting sandstone and redwood house built in 1912. Nearby is a self-guided nature trail. The dirt road, which begins at the parking lot, continues uphill past the campground and climbs nearly 1,700 feet in about 3 miles to Skyline Boulevard near the summit of the ridge. This route offers beautiful views of the Santa

106

The old Welch-Hurst House (1908) has been thoughtfully renovated and is now one of the Bay Area's most attractive and comfortable hostels. It's a wonderful getaway from the city, and a place to meet travelers from around the world.

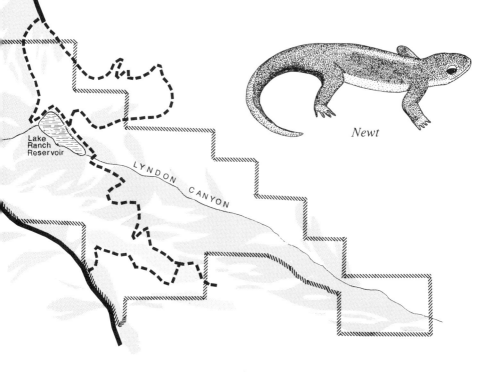

Newt

Lake Ranch Reservoir

LYNDON CANYON

Clara Valley and passes through several different ecological zones. Second-growth redwoods predominate in the shady canyon bottom around park headquarters. Douglas fir, tanoak, bay, and madrone becomes increasingly common in the higher and drier areas where the trail approaches Skyline.

You will probably notice the creeping, climbing wild cucumber plant intertwined with the branches of trees. The Indians used the spiny seed pods of this common vine to cure a variety of ailments, including venereal disease and kidney trouble.

The Sanborn Trail may be used as an extension to the "Skyline-to-the-Sea" trail by parking at the overnight parking lot and hiking west on the Sanborn Trail and north on the Skyline Trail, which connects with Castle Rock State Park. The Castle Rock Trail Camp is an additional 3.2 miles on the Castle Rock Trail, which connects with the "Skyline-to-the-Sea" trail at Saratoga Gap.

The Skyline Trail connects with the Summit Rock Trail which goes to Summit Rock, a sandstone counterpart to Castle Rock and a good place to climb around and explore. It offers a spectacular view of the Santa Clara Valley and has some interesting caves.

This park has one of the most unusual and interesting Youth Hostels in the state. Built of redwood logs, the historic Welch-Hurst House (1908) is about as rustic as anyplace can be, and makes an ideal getaway from the city. Thoughtfully renovated, the inside is comfortable and has many modern conveniences. The log house is in a shadowy grove of redwoods, which also has picnic tables, a barbeque, a wonderful old gazebo, and a duck pond. The hostel is open all year from 5 p.m. to 9 a.m. For more information call (408) 741-9555, or (408) 298-0670.

Lake Ranch Unit

The southern part of this park can be reached by taking Sanborn Road to its southern end. Though this large area has no formal foot trails as of this writing, it is crossed by an eminently hikable dirt road that climbs to a reservoir and levels out and drops before making a steep assault on the Skyline ridge.

From the end of Sanborn Road take the uphill dirt road to the right. The short, but invigorating ascent to Lake Ranch Reservoir is a great destination for a short ramble. You can stop here and have lunch with the newts, who consider this a favorite hangout. The trail continues around the reservoir and drops a little before climbing to Skyline.

The terrain here is steep and the mountains are wooded with bay, Douglas fir, oak, maple, madrone, and redwood. Just east of the dirt road is the canyon abyss of the San Andreas Fault rift zone, where two continental plates collide.

Except for registered camping, the park is open from 8 a.m. until sundown. For more information, call (408) 867-6940.

Model plane flying is one of the activities available at Santa Teresa.

Santa Teresa County Park

TO GET THERE . . . take **Bernal Road southwest from Highway 101**.

Above the south-bounding amorphous sprawl of San Jose, this gentle, grassy park is witness to the dramatic urbanization that is transforming this part of the Santa Clara Valley. Housing tracts and industry sprout at its feet at this narrow part of the valley, making Santa Teresa an important urban recreation area.

Santa Teresa County Park is 1,006 acres of low grassy hills capped by rocky outcroppings which offer views of the Santa Clara Valley immediately below, and Mount Hamilton and the Diablo Range in the distance. The trails here are easy and relaxed; perfect for a picnic.

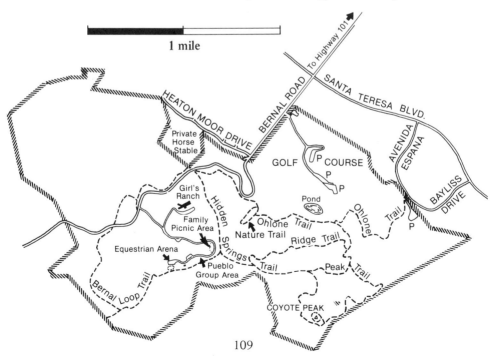

1 mile

Scattered stands of oak and bay punctuate the grassy hills, which turn brilliant green between January and May, yet are roasted brown by late May as if — as John Muir noted — every leaf and blade had been baked in an oven.

This is also one of the best places around to find miners lettuce. Between February and April great green fields of this delicious leafy herb abound. Bring bowls and salad dressing.

Santa Teresa has excellent equestrian trails, lots of group picnic facilities, a fishing pond, a field archery range, an eighteen-hole golf course, and a field for operating radio-controlled miniature airplanes.

For more information, call the park department at (408) 358-3741.

Saratoga Gap Open Space

TO GET THERE . . . the trail through this park can be started at Saratoga Gap near the northeast corner of the intersection of Skyline Boulevard and Highway 9. This trail continues north through Skyline County Park and Monte Bello Open Space.

Saratoga Gap Open Space Preserve is at the northeast corner of Saratoga Gap. The trail through this 492 acre park parallels Skyline Boulevard, crossing grassy hills that explode with wildflowers in early spring. The route then enters 1,165 acre Skyline County Park and dips into the steep, shady canyon that contains the cool and perennial waters of Stevens Creek. You will find many impressive vistas along this trail and see beautiful stands of bay trees, madrone, and canyon live, coast live, and black oak. The Stevens Creek canyon is forested largely with Douglas fir and with big-leaf maple along the creek. The banks of this bouncing, bubbling creek make an excellent picnic stop.

The trail climbs the other slope of the canyon, following a dirt road and rising to the oak and bay studded grasslands of Monte Bello Ridge. Monte Bello Open Space Preserve contains 1,520 acres and can be reached from Saratoga Gap via the trail previously described or from Page Mill Road. The park has a 5 mile trail system on the western slopes of Black Mountain, providing beautiful panoramas, grassy picnicking spots, and amiable old oaks.

There are 3 parks that can be combined to form a grand and diverse hiking adventure of nearly 8 miles from Saratoga Gap to Page Mill Road and Los Trancos Open Space Preserve. Unless you want to hike another 8 miles back, use 2 cars and at least 1 friend and leave a car at Page Mill Road to shuttle back to the trailhead. This hike passes through Saratoga Gap Open Space Preserve, Skyline County Park, and Monte Bello Open Space Preserve. Just north of Page Mill Road is Los Trancos Open Space Preserve. This route explores grassy ridges, chaparral, oak woodlands, and forests of Douglas fir, and involves an elevation range of about 1,400 feet.

"Why preserve open space? Because in the natural world, we find a bond between the past and the future, between our lives and other life. We are humbled and yet exalted, and from that, we find our niche."

—**Kathy Blackburn**

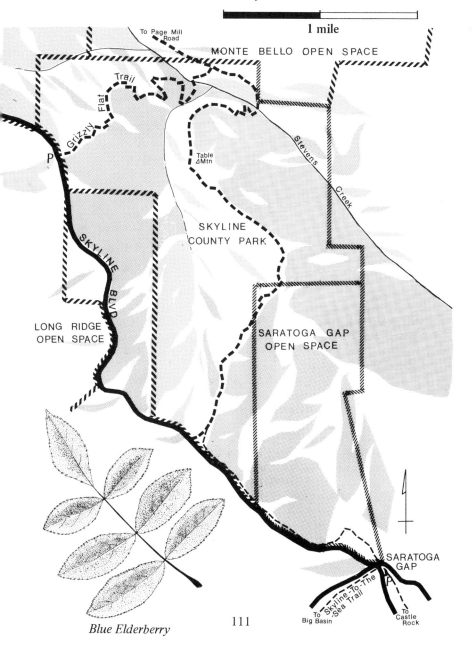

1 mile

To Page Mill Road

MONTE BELLO OPEN SPACE

Grizzly Flat Trail

Table △Mtn

Stevens Creek

SKYLINE COUNTY PARK

SKYLINE BLVD

LONG RIDGE OPEN SPACE

SARATOGA GAP OPEN SPACE

SARATOGA GAP

To Skyline-To-The-Sea Trail

To Big Basin

To Castle Rock

Blue Elderberry

Sierra Azul Open Space

In the rugged and dry part of the Santa Cruz Mountains east of Highway 17, the Sierra Azul (Spanish for "Blue Range") now has public access in 3 units of the 5,294-acre Sierra Azul Open Space. For more information call the Midpeninsula Regional Open Space District at (415) 949-5500.

KENNEDY ROAD AREA:
TO GET THERE . . . take Highway 17 to Los Gatos, head southeast on Saratoga-Los Gatos Road and turn left on Los Gatos Boulevard. Turn right on Kennedy Road and continue about 2.4 miles to the park entrance at its intersection with Top Of The Hill Road. The entrance trail begins just to the left of a private driveway which is across from the intersection.

A well-maintained dirt road serves as a good trail for a climb of about 1600 feet to the top of the ridge.

Along the way you will pass steep and wooded canyons filled with oak, bay, and maple, and views of ever-increasing splendor reveal Mount Hamilton and the Diablo Range, San Jose, and the Santa Clara Valley. The scenery gets increasingly wild and remote as you climb higher on this chaparral-clad ridge.

At the beginning of the trail is an abandoned apricot orchard that still bears a bountiful harvest of delicious fruit around late June and early July. Be prepared for warm weather in summer and little water. Poison oak is common, but easily avoided. This unit covers 467 acres.

LIMEKILN CANYON AREA:
TO GET THERE . . .take Highway 17 south of Los Gatos to the

Lexington Reservoir. Take Alma Bridge Road about 1.6 miles to where the trail begins at a green metal gate.

The 900-foot ascent to Priest Rock begins with the oak woods, but soon enters the nearly shadeless realm of chaparral. During the warm summer months this trail will seem particularly formidable, and unless you bring plenty of water the only moisture you will find anywhere will be perspiration. If you make it to the top and back on a warm day reward yourself with a dip in the reservoir.

The upper parts of this 844-acre unit have few trees, but lots of views. Look for Mount Hamilton, the Santa Clara Valley, San Francisco Bay, and the Skyline Ridge.

In a chaparral area such as this, where dense brush makes travel difficult, wildlife as well as people use the trails and dirt roads. Look for signs of coyotes, deer, bobcats, and others. While walking up this trail I came around a bend and was suddenly confronted with a wild pig and her 5 young.

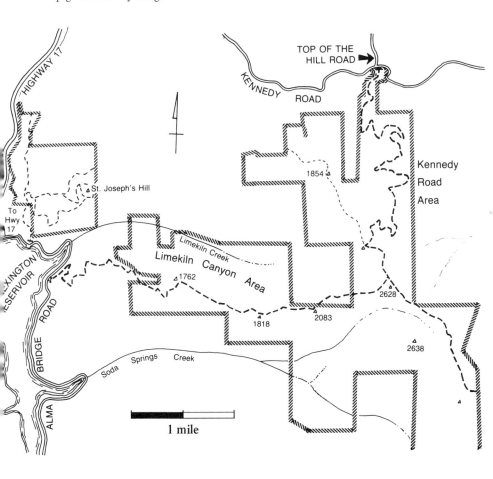

113

MOUNT UMUNHUM AREA:

TO GET THERE. . . from Highway 17 take Camden Road south, turn right on Hicks Road and continue 6.3 miles to where it intersects Mount Umunhum Road. Take this private road uphill, to the west, 1.8 miles and park near the stop sign at the locked gate.

This rugged land of steep ravines and breathtaking views forms a 2,840-acre patchwork of open space astride the Sierra Azul Range.

Unfortunately for trail users the only access through the preserve and to the 3,486-foot summit of Mount Umunhum is by way of a two-lane paved road built by the U.S. Air Force on a non-exclusive easement over private land. It provided access to the radar tower of the former Almaden Air Force Station on Mount Umunhum. Though it passes through private land, the open space district maintains that the public has a right to use it to get to open space property. Because some local property owners dispute this claim, visitors are encouraged to call the open space district office for current information.

Mount Umunhum, one of the most prominent features of the Santa Cruz Mountains, means hummingbird in the Ohlone Indian language and was considered to be one of their 4 sacred Bay Area peaks.

The Bald Mountain parcel of this preserve is easily accessible to

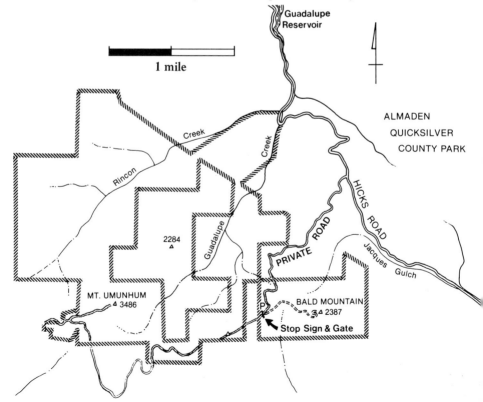

114

the public without walking on asphalt. Park just off the road near the stop sign at the locked gate and follow the dirt road that heads to the southeast and up the grassy hilltop. This 2,387-foot rounded summit is an easy half-mile walk to a place that is perfect for picnicking and kite flying. It is also one of the few places in the vicinity not covered with chaparral. Dramatic views of the Sierra Azul Range and the Santa Clara Valley are among the best reasons to visit.

For more information call the Midpeninsula Regional Open Space District at (415) 949-5500.

Skyline Ridge Open Space

TO GET THERE . . . from Highway 280 take Page Mill Road uphill and west to where it intersects Skyline Boulevard and turns into Alpine Road. The preserve begins at the southwest corner of the intersection. Another access is at the gate to the Christmas tree farm about a mile south of the Alpine/Skyline intersection.

This is a walkers' paradise, with an excellent ranch road trail system that passes by several beautiful reservoirs, wanders through shady forests, and climbs high, scenic ridgetops.

A few of the major trails are on the map; but there are many other paths that fit together into a nearly infinite combination of possible routes. The best advice is to go there and walk. Explore the pond at the Alpine/Skyline access, and turn right (west) for a gradual downhill ramble through oak, madrone, and Douglas fir woodlands. The original Page Mill Road west of Skyline, built in the nineteenth century for hauling redwood lumber, runs through here as a dirt road.

For a more uplifting walk, head left (east) and take the ranch road uphill to the highest point in the preserve at 2,493 feet. The view into the steep canyon below is truly breathtaking. Continuing east, you will walk by contorted old oaks, and through grassy fields and neat rows of Christmas trees.

One of the best things about the southeast part of the preserve is springfed Horseshoe Lake, probably named because of its shape. With good water quality, this 27-foot deep pond is inhabited by bluegill and bass.

As of this writing the open space district has big plans for this preserve, including camping, fishing, equestrian facilities, and maybe even a hostel. Because of its magnificent setting and easy connection with other preserves the district wants to make Skyline Ridge an open space showcase as the Christmas tree farms are phased out.

The easiest entry into this part of the preserve is at a gate into the Christmas tree farm, on Skyline just over a mile south of Alpine Road.

Though the land is being cultivated by private tree farmers who lease 123 acres, this is still public parkland; so walk right through. Take one of the dirt road trails down to Horsehoe Lake. Just west of the lake an intersecting trail veers to the south and climbs past another Christmas tree grove and uphill further to the splendid panorama at the highest point in the preserve. From here you can see thousands of feet down into the Peters Creek canyon to the west; Loma Prieta, the highest peak in the range, to the south; and Monte Bello Ridge and Mount Diablo to the east.

This 1254-acre preserve is an important part of the Skyline open space corridor, and will be a key link in the developing Skyline Corridor Trail through San Mateo and Santa Clara counties. This park is part of more than 7,500 acres of contiguous open space and parkland on the Skyline Ridge area. For more information, call the Midpeninsula Regional Open Space District (415) 949-5500.

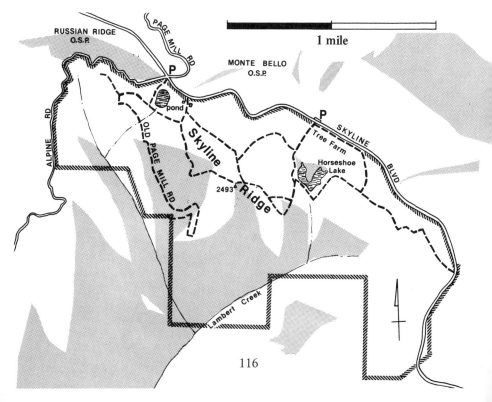

116

This grand old oak is at Skyline Ridge Open Space.

The Santa Cruz Mountains have many noble stands of oak and bay for pursuing the challenging sport of tree climbing. This sport offers all the fun of rock climbing, but with a lot more hand and foot holds and no need for technical aides.

First, you need to know which trees are most climbable. Redwoods and other conifers are usually out of the question because they are too straight and have no low-lying branches. Madrones are sometimes suitable, but their surfaces are usually too smooth to find hand and foot holds.

Oaks of any variety are the best climbing trees, especially those old ones with thick trunks, deep furrowed bark, and large contorted branches that nearly touch the ground. You can climb around like an ape, with never a lack of something to hold on to for support. Bay trees also make great arboreal jungle gyms, and the older and more gnarled the better.

A: Sanborn Hostel
B: Sanborn Campground
C: Castle Rock Trailcamp
D: Waterman Gap Trailcamp
E: Big Basin "J" Camp
F: Lane Trailcamp
G: Camp Herbert Trailcamp
H: Twin Redwoods Trailcamp
I: Alder Trailcamp
J: Sunset Trailcamp

Skyline-to-the-Sea Trail

TO GET THERE ... the trail begins at the intersection of Skyline and Highway 9, or at Highway 1 at Waddell Creek. It can be extended through Castle Rock State Park, Sanborn Skyline County Park, and Monte Bello open space.

Skyline to Big Basin

The "Skyline-to-the-Sea" trail gives hikers a chance to do some real backpacking from Saratoga Gap or Castle Rock State Park to Big Basin Redwoods State Park and on to the coast.

The total distance from Saratoga Gap to the ocean is about 28 miles. The trail passes through grasslands, chaparral, and forests of oak, madrone, Douglas fir and redwoods, and impressive vistas are common along the route.

The trailhead at Saratoga Gap (where Skyline Boulevard intersects Highway 9) is on the south side of Highway 9 just west of Skyline. From the Castle Rock State Park trailcamp the trail crosses Skyline twice before connecting the main trail at Saratoga Gap. The trail parallels Highway 9 for about 8 miles from Saratoga Gap to Waterman Gap campground. The distance to Waterman Gap from the Castle Rock trailhead is about 15.5 miles.

The "Skyline-to-the-Sea" trail, which was built by thousands of volunteers in 1969, closely parallels highways 9 and 236 because this land was already owned by the state. Hikers who prefer straying farther from the sound of traffic should try hiking the Toll Road south of Highway 9. This abandoned logging road, built in 1870, connects with the main "Skyline-to-the-Sea" route west of Saratoga Gap and again west of the junction of Highways 9 and 236.

The trail continues for about 9.5 miles from Waterman Gap to Big Basin Park Headquarters. Take the Soroptimist-Opal Creek Trail from China Grade. Hikers should be aware that starting the trail at Castle Rock adds 7.5 miles to the total distance to Big Basin. From China Grade Road the trail passes through chaparral and stands of knobcone pine and enters the shady redwood groves along Opal Creek. Just before the trail drops into Big Basin you will be greeted by splendid views of the mountains to the southwest, and on clear days you may also get a glimpse of the ocean.

Due to a lack of water on parts of the trail during the dry season, hikers are advised to bring water. The Castle Rock campground has water, pit toilets, and fireplaces. The Waterman Gap campground has water, pit toilets, and does not permit ground fires. The Big Basin "J" camp has water, flush toilets, fireplaces, and showers. Campsite reservations may be made in person, by phone, or by mail up to 90 days in advance at Big Basin. Call (408) 338-6132.

Big Basin to the Sea

The new "Big Basin-to-the-Sea" trail follows Waddell Creek through the 1,700 acre "Rancho Del Oso" property, which connects the state park with the coast. This trail can be found by taking the Berry Creek Falls Trail to near the confluence of Waddell and Berry creeks, and by following Waddell Creek downstream. The distance from park headquarters to Highway 1 is about 10.5 miles on the Berry Creek Falls Trail, about 11 miles on the Howard King Trail, and about 12 miles on the Sunset Trail. The Berry Creek Trail has the easiest grade of these three routes. Hikers taking the Sunset Trail may want to make camp at the Sunset Trailcamp, which is about a quarter mile east of Berry Creek and upstream from Golden Falls.

There are 3 trailcamps in "Rancho Del Oso": Camp Herbert is about 7.5 miles from Big Basin park headquarters; Twin Redwoods is 1.5 miles downstream from Camp Herbert; and Alder Camp is less than a mile downstream from Alder Camp. Ground fires are prohibited and campers are encouraged to make reservations by calling Big Basin park headquarters at (408) 338-6132.

Racoons are a common delight, but they can be a problem for backpackers. Usually nocturnal, they eat almost anything they can get their little paws on, including your food. If you're bothered by hungry racoons at night, throw a rope over a tree branch and hoist your food out of their reach.

This beautiful canyon was an ideal place for the Ohlone Indians, who gathered marine edibles from the coast and stalked game in the mountains. Mammals you may see here include coyotes, racoons, deer, bobcats, foxes, weasels, possums, skunks, several species of squirrels, chipmunks, and an assortment of other rodents. Bears no longer roam these mountains and mountain lions are rare. This is still an important feeding and nesting area for birds, with more than 200 species sighted. Near the trail is the Eagle Tree, an impressive first-growth redwood which once hosted an eagle nest.

The old "Big Basin-to-the-Sea" trail may still be used by taking the Sunset Trail to the Sunset Trailcamp and west to a ridgetop fire road that continues to the coast on Whitehouse Creek Road. This dirt road goes through Cascade Ranch State Park. Sunset Camp is 5.5 miles from park headquarters and has water, pit toilets, and prohibits ground fires.

Detailed topographic maps of the "Skyline-to-the-Sea" trail are available from the Sempervirens Fund at P.O. Box 1141, Los Altos, CA 94022; (415) 968-4509.

The "Skyline-to-the-Sea" trail is the hub of a vast network of trails developing in this part of the Santa Cruz Mountains. It is now possible to hike about 8.5 miles from Los Trancos Open Space Preserve on Page Mill Road to Saratoga Gap, where you can connect with the "Skyline-to-the-Sea" trail. To hike from one side of the range to the other, park at Sanborn-Skyline County Park and take the Sanborn and Skyline trails to Castle Rock State Park and on to Saratoga Gap via the Castle Rock Trail.

A new trail is now being built between Big Basin and Portola state parks. The Olmo Fire Trail goes from Butano State Park to the China Grade Road in Big Basin, though public access to this route is still disputed. See the appropriate chapters for more detailed information on these connecting trails.

See the Big Basin and Castle Rock chapters for more detailed maps and information.

Tourists at Big Basin in the 1920s.

Conservationists have been active in the Santa Cruz Mountains since the beginning of this century, when San Jose photographer Andrew P. Hill (1853-1922) started a movement to establish California's first state park at Big Basin in 1901. Angered by unrestricted logging, he founded the Sempervirens Club to protect the outstanding natural beauty of the area.

Hill's work continues today as the Sempervirens Fund, a non-profit organization which raises funds for the completion of Castle Rock and Big Basin state parks. They also help to build trails and plant trees in the two parks. To participate, write to: Sempervirens Fund, P.O. Box 1141, Los Altos, California 94022.

Uvas Canyon County Park

TO GET THERE. . . take Croy Road west from Uvas Road. It's west of Morgan Hill.

This 1,049-acre wooded park is tucked into a beautiful canyon west of Morgan Hill. Here you can escape the crowds and hike about 7 miles of trails along shady creeks and through wonderfully diverse forests of second-growth redwood, Douglas fir, bay, madrone, sycamore, bigleaf maple, buckeye, and several kinds of oak.

A great day hike can be taken on the loop trail beginning at the "nature trail" about a quarter mile beyond the bridge on the left side of the road. Follow the Swanson Creek Trail until it crosses Swanson Creek beyond the Old Hot House Site. This part of the route becomes the Contour Trail, which gains elevation and eventually intersects Alec Canyon Trail. Turn left here and return to the starting point. This loop is only about 3 easy miles and involves just a little uphill hiking. Short sidetrips from the loop trail can be made to Black Rock Falls and Basin Falls.

For a more vigorous walk, climb Nibbs Knob by way of the Nibbs Knob Fire Trail. This 3-mile round trip climbs more than 1,400 feet for a commanding panorama of the region.

The park has a family campground, available on a first-come, first-serve basis, and picnic facilities. For more information, call (408) 779-9232.

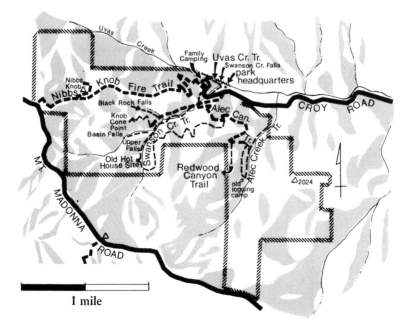

Villa Montalvo

TO GET THERE... take Saratoga-Los Gatos Road south of Highway 9 in Saratoga and turn southwest on Montalvo Road.

Villa Montalvo is a 175 acre cultural center, arboretum, and wildlife refuge in the hills west of Saratoga. The mansion is maintained by the Montalvo Association, and the remainder of the grounds have been under Santa Clara County jurisdiction since 1960.

Villa Montalvo is a very unique park. Because it is more of an educational than a recreational facility, there are no picnicking or camping facilities available. An easy 1.5 mile self-guided nature loop climbs about 400 feet into the Santa Cruz Mountains foothills. The park has only about 3 miles of trails, making it a good place for casual hikes and an excellent place to study the ecology of the east side of the Santa Cruz Mountains.

You can tell a lot about an area by the relationship between grasslands and oak trees. Oaks don't die out during the summer dry spell as do the annual grasses, and though they have deeper roots than the grasses, they need a lot more moisture to survive. A dense stand of oaks is an indication of available ground water, while a wide spacing of trees tells us that underground water is scarce and must be conserved among trees.

The arboretum is open to the public from 1 a.m. to 5 p.m. and the mansion is open from 1 p.m. to 4 p.m. The grounds and mansion were bought by California Senator and San Francisco Mayor James Phelan in 1911. Rooms on the estate are now rented to promising artists.

For more information, call (408) 867-0190.

Wilder Ranch State Park

TO GET THERE. . . it's just west of Santa Cruz, continuing along both sides of Highway 1 for about 3½ miles.

This park sprawls over 5,000 acres of beaches, grasslands, oak-woods, redwood groves, and brussels sprouts fields. It is scheduled to open to the public in the summer of 1988 after the restoration of several historic buildings, the marking of trails, and the completion of a parking lot and ranger station. Be sure to call for current information before visiting.

This land was once the Wilder Ranch, a prosperous dairy operation headquartered in a cluster of 19th-century buildings just off Highway 1. The oldest of these structures is an 1830's adobe built when this was Rancho Refugio, a Mexican land grant. A workshop with water-powered machinery, a dairy barn built of hand-hewn timbers held together with

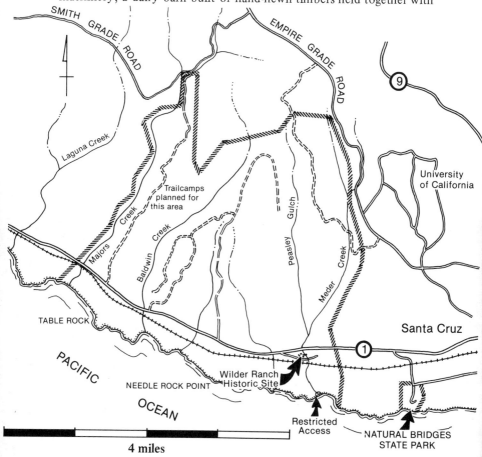

Antique agricultural methods are sometimes demonstrated at Wilder Ranch. The 1891 horse barn is in the background.

Candida and Jose Antonio Bolcoff raised 11 children in this small adobe, which they built in the 1830's. It was then part of a huge Mexican land grant called Rancho Refugio.

wooden pegs, a horse barn, 2 houses, and several other historic buildings remain from the period before 1900. These buildings are in the process of being restored for use as a park interpretive center and agricultural history exhibit.

After nearly a century of family ownership, the Wilders sold the ranch in the late 1960's to a development company which intended to convert the land to housing and commercial facilities. But when public opposition doomed this plan the state purchased the property in 1975, though it is only now starting to become publicly accessible.

Several areas will continue to have restricted public access, including a beach used for nesting snowy plovers, the marsh at the mouth of Meder Creek, and about 600 acres of farmland that will be kept in brussells sprouts. Cattle will probably continue to graze grassland areas.

Among the park's natural assets is an old-growth grove of redwoods along the headwaters of Majors Creek which was purchased by the Save the Redwoods League.

A beautiful natural beach grotto carpeted with ferns is one of the main attractions along the coast.

Long-term plans include a drive-in campground along Highway 1 and several trailcamps in the backcountry.

For current information call the state parks regional office at (408) 688-3241 or Natural Bridges State Park at (408) 423-4609. Also contact Friends of Wilder Ranch, 1401 Post Road, Santa Cruz, CA 95060.

Windy Hill Open Space

TO GET THERE. . . take Skyline Boulevard 5 miles north of the Page Mill intersection and 2.3 miles south of the Woodside Road intersection. Park at the picnic area on the east side of Skyline.

If ever a hill lived up to its name, this is it. In fact, this preserve includes an area of high, grassy hills, seen from much of the Bay Area and exposed to the currents of wind that wash in from the coast. The preserve has about 10 miles of trails, several of which combine to form a fairly strenuous 8.4-mile loop from Skyline Boulevard parking lot to Alpine Road and back.

Take the foot trail from the picnic table area to the slope of Windy Hill itself and make a hardy ascent to the top. Here you will find one of the Santa Cruz Mountains' great views, with the bay and its cities spread out below. This windswept point is perfect for kite flying, with no entangling trees or telephone wires.

If you grow tired of the wind, follow the footpath as it contours

This is a good place to fly radio-controlled gliders.

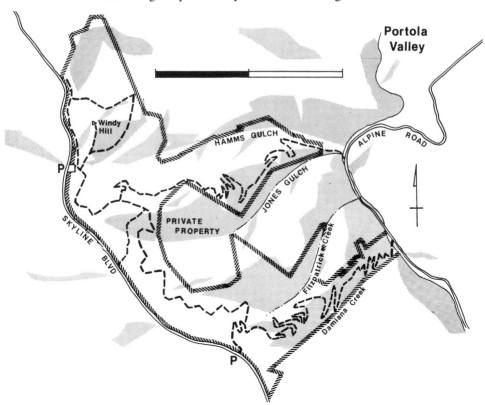

the hill and descends to a quiet and shady little grove of Monterey Cypress. The western slopes of Windy Hill have been designated a soaring area, for use by non-motorized model gliders. For more information, write: South Bay Soaring Society, P.O. Box 2012, Sunnyvale, CA 94087.

The southern part of the preserve is largely covered with chaparral, and madrone, bay, and Douglas fir woodlands. To explore this area, walk or drive just under a mile from the picnic area to the gate at the dirt road that intersects Skyline. Either walk on the maintained dirt road, or turn south just beyond the gate on the deteriorated old ranch roads.

Windy Hill was donated to the Midpeninsula Regional Open Space District with the help of the Peninsula Open Space Trust, which works with private landowners for protecting baylands, the San Mateo County coast, and the Skyline scenic corridor.

Dogs on leash are allowed in designated areas.

Wunderlich County Park

TO GET THERE... take Woodside Road west from Interstate 280. Turn in at the parking lot at 4040 Woodside Road, about 2 miles southwest of the town of Woodside.

This is one of the most ecologically diverse and scenically beautiful parks east of Skyline. It's well used by equestrians, but there are surprisingly few hikers enjoying the park's 942 acres.

From the park entrance parking lot, at the Folger Ranch buildings, this looks like an oakwood-brushland park. But a hike up the hillside reveals dark, cool groves of second-growth redwoods, open grassy meadows, and nearly pure stands of Douglas fir. This is a steep park, with an elevation range of more than 1,650 feet; but it has excellent trails that are graded to avoid excessively strenuous climbs.

A beautiful half day, 4.75 mile (7.6 kilometers), hike can be taken by combining the Bear Gulch and Alambique trails. From the parking lot hike uphill on Bear Gulch Trail, passing through live oak groves and pockets of redwoods in shady creek beds.

Along the trail stands the rotting remains of a fence built when Simon Jones owned the property in the latter part of the last century. You will also find a long trough running up the hill. This is one of several skid trails created by oxen dragging redwood logs down the mountain between about 1850 and 1865 to provide lumber for Bay Area cities. The forest has re-grown, but this furrow will probably remain for centuries. You will also see large Douglas fir trees with low sprawling branches, indicating that at one time these trees were in open meadowland which was overgrown with trees when cattle grazing ceased.

Suddenly the forests give way to a beautiful meadow, covered with native bunch grasses and introduced perennials. Around the edges of this grassland stand large climbable oaks, and there are sweeping views that make this a great place to stop and relax for awhile.

The Alambique Trail heads downhill, through all the park's native plant communities, and passing such introduced species as Monterey cyprus, eucalyptus, and olive trees. Be sure to pause and admire the enormous first-growth redwood on the north side of the trail — the kind you wouldn't expect to see east of Skyline. You will also see the ruins of old ninteenth century wagon bridges along the way.

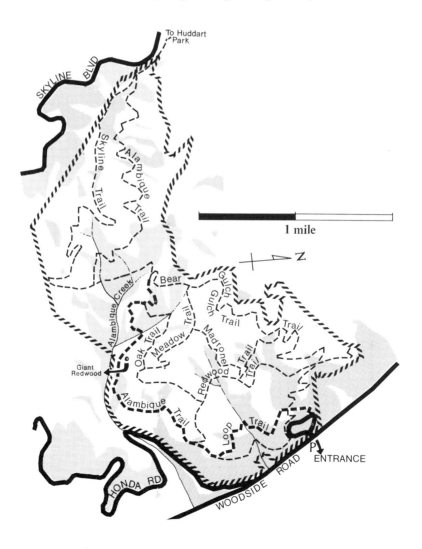

If you have all day or more than the usual amount of energy, hike the 5 mile (8 kilometers) round trip from the meadows to Skyline and back. From Bear Gulch Trail, hike uphill on Alambique Trail to the top of the ridge and then gambol down the Skyline Trail and back to Alambique Creek, which flows along the course of a branch of Pilarcitos Fault. Notice that the rock suddenly changes from sandstone to shale as you cross the fault. Also notice that Douglas fir increasingly forests the steep hillside as you climb towards the Skyline ridge.

Hikers should be aware that this park is heavily used for horse riding and that it is sometimes necessary to watch where you are stepping. You should also be warned that all the trail signs have distances listed in metric units. Remember, there are 1.609 kilometers to a mile.

This park is open for day use only. For more information, call the San Mateo County Parks Department at (415) 364-5600.

See page 63 for details on the Skyline Trail to Huddart Park.

A coyote, chasing a lizard, suddenly changes directions to go after a ground squirrel.

Looking For Signs Of Wildlife

One of the best-kept secrets about the Santa Cruz Mountains is that the place abounds with wildlife. Many visitors complain that they see few wild animals and mistakenly conclude that there aren't many.

The first thing you need to know about most wild animals, especially mammals, is that they don't want to be seen. Plant eaters try to hide from meat eaters and meat eaters try to sneak up on plant eaters. So without exceptionally well-developed powers of observation you could easily walk right past animals and their signs and see nothing.

To make matters worse for wildlife watchers, many wild animals are mainly active at night.

Written records from early settlers and explorers indicate that before the presence of firearms, many native creatures were much more active during the day than they are now, and they were also much less wary of man. With the advent of guns these animals learned to regard us as enemies. Our alienation from wildlife became nearly complete as people settled in farms and then cities and abandoned the prehistoric skills that gave our ancient ancestors a feeling of kinship with the non-human world.

Learning to see and interpret the signs of wildlife is a step toward making a personal peace with nature.

One of the first things you will notice is that wild animals, like people, usually prefer to travel on trails, including those built for human use. Like us, they prefer to take the easiest route to their destination.

I have found that the best places to look for wildlife tracks are on trails or dirt roads where the soil is soft. Tracks can often be seen along the trail edge in dust, but the most clearly defined prints are formed in mud. Look for tracks soon after a rain, especially where the trail dips and soft mud accumulates. If the trail is popular with walkers and equestrians check it out early on a Saturday morning, before the tracks have been stepped on. Moist stream banks are also good places to look.

Serious students of tracking will be able to determine the species, rate of speed, age, and perhaps the goal and intentions of the animals making the tracks. Predators stalking a meal, for example, will have a short stride with their weight heavily shifted toward their toes. Experienced trackers can even tell an animal's gender.

Other signs of wildlife to look for include droppings, scratch marks, burrows, and gnaw marks, to mention a few.

There isn't room in this book to go into much more detail about tracking, but here are 2 books that contain nearly all there is to know on the subject: *Tom Brown's Field Guide To Nature Observation And Tracking,* by Tom Brown, Jr. (Berkley Books, New York, 1983); and *A Field Guide To Animal Tracks,* by Olaus J. Murie (Houghton Mifflin Company, Boston, 1974).

Wildlife Tracks Measured in Inches:

	FRONT TRACK WIDTH	FRONT TRACK LENGTH	REAR TRACK WIDTH	REAR TRACK LENGTH	SPACING BETWEEN TRACKS SLOW STRIDE	SPACING BETWEEN TRACKS FAST STRIDE
Badger	2	2 1/8	2	2	9-12	12-24
Bobcat	1 3/4	1 7/8	1 1/2	1 1/2	7	12-40
Cottontail	5/8	7/8	1 1/8	2 3/4	7-12	15-36
Coyote	2 1/8	2 5/8	2	2 3/4	13-16	16-50
Deer	2 5/8	3 1/4	2 1/2	3 1/8	21-24	72-180
Gray Fox	1 3/8	1 5/8	1 1/4	1 1/2	8-12	18-36
Gray Squirrel	1 3/8	2		1 1/4	2 3/8	10-15	16-38
Ground Squirrel	3/8	5/8	5/8	7/8	2-7	7-15
Jack Rabbit	1 1/8	1 1/2	2	2 3/4	9-12	48-144
Mountain Lion	3 1/2	3 1/4	3 1/4	3	14-17	36-72
Opossum	2	1 7/8	2 1/4	2 1/2	7-10	10-15
Raccoon	3	3	3 3/8	3 3/4	12-16	16-28
Spotted Skunk	1	7/8	1 1/4	1 1/4	4-6	8-12
Striped Skunk	1 1/8	7/8	1 1/2	1 1/2	5-8	10-18

Wildlife Tracks

Most wild animals avoid people, but their tracks are often seen in muddy and dusty places. Here are some tracks you are likely to see in the Santa Cruz Mountains:

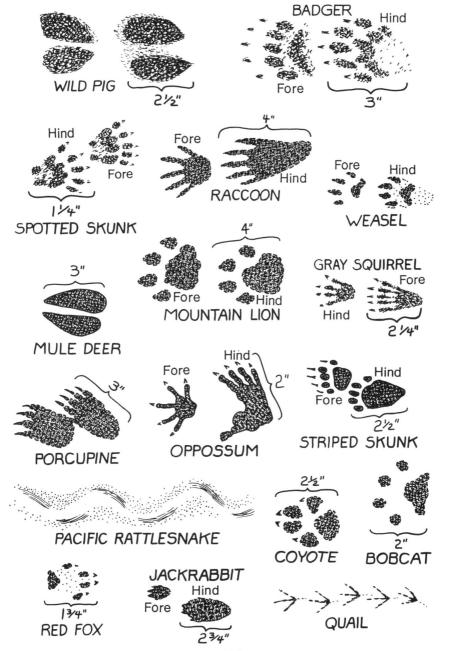

WILD PIG 2½"

BADGER Hind Fore 3"

Hind Fore SPOTTED SKUNK 1¼"

Fore Hind RACCOON 4"

Fore Hind WEASEL

3" MULE DEER

Fore Hind MOUNTAIN LION 4"

GRAY SQUIRREL Fore Hind 2¼"

PORCUPINE 3"

Fore Hind OPPOSSUM 2"

Hind Fore STRIPED SKUNK 2½"

PACIFIC RATTLESNAKE

COYOTE 2½" BOBCAT 2"

RED FOX 1¾"

JACKRABBIT Hind Fore 2¾"

QUAIL

133

Organizations and Agencies

Año Nuevo Interpretive Association: (Natural history); 95 Kelly Ave., Half Moon Bay, CA 94019; (415) 726-6238.

Audubon Society: (Outings and conservation); Santa Clara valley Chapter: 2253 Park Blvd., Palo Alto, CA 94306; (415) 328-5315; Sequoia Chapter: 720 El Camino Real, Belmont, CA 94002; (415) 593-7368.

Bay Area Mountain Watch: (Protection of San Bruno Mountain); P.O. Box AO, Brisbane, CA 94005.

California State Parks Department: (Santa Cruz Mountains Regional Office); Henry Cowell Redwoods State Park, Felton, CA 95018; (408) 335-9106.

Committee For Green Foothills: (Conservation); 2253 Park Blvd., Palo Alto, CA 94306; (415) 328-5313.

Coyote Point Museum: (Environmental Education); Coyote Point, San Mateo, CA 94401; (415) 342-7755.

Environmental Volunteers: (Nature education for children); 2253 Park Blvd., Palo Alto, CA 94306; (415) 327-6017.

Hidden Villa Association: (Environmental education and hostel); 26870 Moody Rd., Los Altos Hills, CA 94022; (415) 941-6119.

Midpeninsula Regional Open Space District: (Docent walks and open space information); Building C, Suite 135/201 San Antonio Circle, Mountain View, CA 94040; (415) 949-5500.

Mountain View Parks Department: (Deer Hollow Farm); 201 S. Rengstorff Ave., Mountain View, CA 94040; (415) 966-6331.

Nature Explorations: (Outings and nature study); 2253 Park Blvd., Palo Alto, CA 94306; (415) 324-8737.

Peninsula Conservation Center: (Conservation activities and environmental library); 2253 Park Blvd., Palo Alto, CA 94306; (415) 328-5313.

Peninsula Open Space Trust: (Acquisition and protection of open space); 3000 Sand Hill Rd., Menlo Park, CA 94025; (415) 854-7696.

San Mateo County Parks Department: County Office Building, Redwood City, CA 94063; (415) 363-4021;

Santa Clara County Parks Department: 298 Garden Hill Dr., Los Gatos, CA 95030; (408) 358-3751.

The Santa Cruz Mountains Natural History Association: (Nature education); 101 North Big Trees Rd., Felton, CA 95018; (408) 335-5858.

The Santa Cruz Mountains Trail Association: (Trail building and maintenance); P.O. Box 1141, Los Altos, CA 94022.

Sempervirens Fund: (Parkland acquisition); P.O. Box 1141, Los Altos, CA 94022; (415) 968-4509.

Sierra Club: (Outings and conservation); Loma Prieta Chapter: 2253 Park Blvd., Palo Alto, CA 94306; (415) 327-8111.

Trail Center: (Trail building, maintenance, and information); 4898 El Camino Real, Office 205A, Los Altos, CA 94022; (415) 968-7065.

Santa Cruz Mountains Trees

MONTEREY CYPRESS
Grows mainly along coast.

DOUGLAS FIR
One of the most common trees in the range.

KNOBCONE PINE
Found on dry, rocky ridgetops.

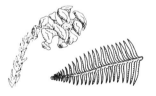

CALIFORNIA NUTMEG
Stiff, sharp needles.

REDWOOD
Flourishes in moist canyon bottoms. Found mostly on the west side of the range.

CALIFORNIA BLACK OAK
Often found on ridges on the east side of the range.

BLUE OAK
Grows on the dry east side of the mountain.

COAST LIVE OAK
Drought resistant. Common on dry hillsides.

INTERIOR LIVE OAK
Grows as a shrub with chaparral or as a tree on wooded hillsides.

TANOAK
Often grows on ridges and mixed with redwood and Douglas fir.

CALIFORNIA WHITE OAK
Common at low elevations east of Skyline.

OREGON WHITE OAK
Found mostly on dry ridges.

RED ALDER
Riperian tree.

OREGON ASH

BAY TREE
Common on the east side of
the range. Leaves are fragrant
and used for seasoning.

BLUEBLOSSOM
Grows in moist, wooded areas.

BLUE ELDERBERRY
Found mostly on the east side
of the range. Often grows with
chaparral.

BOXELDER
Found on low hills and creekbeds.

CALIFORNIA BUCKEYE
Common on east side of the
range. Leaves drop in summer
and reappear in February.

CHRISTMASBERRY TOYON
Common in dry areas. Red
berries appear in winter.

BLACK COTTONWOOD
Found in streamside wood-
lands.

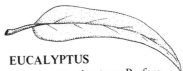

EUCALYPTUS
Large non-native tree. Prefers
low elevations.

PACIFIC DOGWOOD
Grows along creeks.

CALIFORNIA HAZEL
Small understory tree. Shade tolerant.

BIGLEAF MAPLE
Loses leaves in late fall.

MADRONE
Common on dry ridges. Bark peels.

WAX MYRTLE
A small coastal creekside tree.

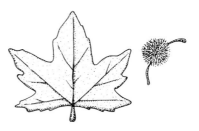

CALIFORNIA SYCAMORE
Found mostly near creeks.

HINDS WALNUT

ARROYO WILLOW
Common streamside tree.

Uncle Tom's Acorn Muffins

Acorns were the staff of life for the Ohlone Indians, the one food they ate nearly every day of their lives. The autumn acorn harvest was so important it marked the beginning and end of each year.

Though the Ohlone usually ate their acorns as a mush, here is a muffin recipe more suited to our tastes:

First, shell the acorns, placing the nuts in hot water. Let them sit until the water turns brown, and then repeat until the water is only a pale brown. Then put the acorns in a blender and gradually add only as much water as is needed to blend them into a mush.

Pour the acorn mush into a bowl and stir in the honey/brown sugar, shortening, eggs, all-purpose flour, baking powder, raisins, and milk.

Bake in muffin pans at 400 degrees F. for about 20 minutes.

> *1 cup acorn mush*
> *4 tablespoons brown sugar or honey*
> *3 tablespoons melted shortening*
> *2 eggs beaten*
> *1 cup sifted all-purpose flour*
> *2½ teaspoons baking powder*
> *½ cup raisins*
> *¾ cup of milk*

Makes 12-14 muffins.